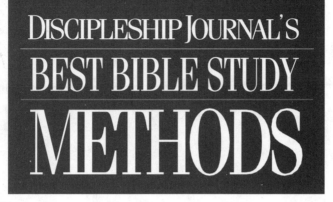

DISCIPLESHIP JOURNAL'S
BEST BIBLE STUDY
METHODS

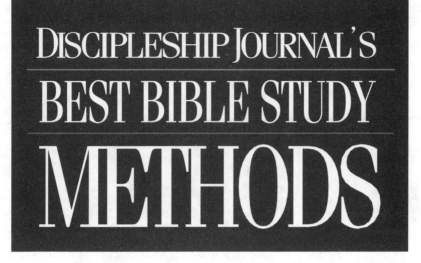

DISCIPLESHIP JOURNAL'S
BEST BIBLE STUDY
METHODS

COMPILED BY
MELISSA MUNRO AND
JUDITH COUCHMAN

NAVPRESS

Bringing Truth to Life
P.O. Box 35001, Colorado Springs, Colorado 80935

OUR GUARANTEE TO YOU

We believe so strongly in the message of our books that we are making this quality guarantee to you. If for any reason you are disappointed with the content of this book, return the title page to us with your name and address and we will refund to you the list price of the book. To help us serve you better, please briefly describe why you were disappointed. Mail your refund request to: NavPress, P.O. Box 35002, Colorado Springs, CO 80935.

The Navigators is an international Christian organization. Our mission is to reach, disciple, and equip people to know Christ and to make Him known through successive generations. We envision multitudes of diverse people in the United States and every other nation who have a passionate love for Christ, live a lifestyle of sharing Christ's love, and multiply spiritual laborers among those without Christ.

NavPress is the publishing ministry of The Navigators. NavPress publications help believers learn biblical truth and apply what they learn to their lives and ministries. Our mission is to stimulate spiritual formation among our readers.

ISBN 1-57683-291-0

Cover design by Ray Moore
Cover illustration by Jim Dryden
Creative Team: Paul Santhouse, Greg Clouse, Melissa Munro, Darla Hightower, Pat Miller

Some of the anecdotal illustrations in this book are true to life and are included with the permission of the persons involved. All other illustrations are composites of real situations, and any resemblance to people living or dead is coincidental.

Unless otherwise identified, all Scripture quotations in this publication are taken from the *HOLY BIBLE: NEW INTERNATIONAL VERSION®* (NIV®). Copyright © 1973, 1978, 1984 by International Bible Society. Used by permission of Zondervan Publishing House. All rights reserved. Other versions include the *New American Standard Bible* (NASB), © The Lockman Foundation 1960, 1962, 1963, 1968, 1971, 1972, 1973, 1975, 1977, 1995; the *New Revised Standard Version* (NRSV), copyright © 1989, by the Division of Christian Education of the National Council of the Churches of Christ in the USA, used by permission, all rights reserved; the *New King James Version* (NKJV), copyright © 1979, 1980, 1982, 1990, Thomas Nelson Inc., Publishers; the *King James Version* (KJV); and the Contemporary English Version (CEV), copyright © 1991, American Bible Society.

CIP DATA APPLIED FOR

Printed in the United States of America

1 2 3 4 5 6 7 8 9 10 / 05 04 03 02

FOR A FREE CATALOG OF
NAVPRESS BOOKS & BIBLE STUDIES,
CALL 1-800-366-7788 (USA)
OR 1-416-499-4615 (CANADA)

Contents

PART FOUR: Live What You Learn
APPLY BIBLICAL PRINCIPLES TO YOUR EVERYDAY LIFE.

Introduction

Getting Into God's Word

I committed my life to Christ halfway through the book of Acts. When curiosity propels you to a bookstore to buy a Bible . . . and when you meet your Savior in its pages. . . well, you are almost destined to have a special relationship with the Word of God.

Shortly after I met Christ in the pages of a paperback Bible, I heard about a new magazine called *Discipleship Journal.* I subscribed immediately, and it became one of my early guides through Scripture. Long before I became its editor, I was an eager reader who learned from its pages how to understand Scripture and apply it to my daily life.

About eleven years later, I joined its staff. Shortly after that, we created a new department for our readers. Bible Study Methods debuted in 1994 with the ABC Method. Since then, we've steered *DJ* readers through thirty-minute Bible study methods and thirty-day methods, through studies on a single book and studies that overview the entire Bible, through studies that appeal to left-brainers and studies that capture the imaginations of right-brainers, through studies for individuals and studies for small groups.

About five years after we started the Bible Study Methods department, we changed its name to Getting Into God's Word and expanded its range to include ideas for personal devotions as well as more intense study. Many of those methods have now been compiled for you in this NavPress book. Whether you've been studying Scripture for years or are a rookie, you'll find ideas here for discovering the literary richness of the Bible, delving into the meanings behind its word pictures and poetry, or building a better understanding of key biblical themes.

No matter which of these methods you choose to explore, be prepared. The Bible is a book that changes lives. It dramatically changed mine nearly twenty-five years ago and continues to work its persistent transformation day after day after day. May it do the same for you.

Sue Kline is the editor of *Discipleship Journal.*
You can write to the *Discipleship Journal* editor at sue.kline@navpress.com.
Visit the magazine on the web at www.discipleshipjournal.com.

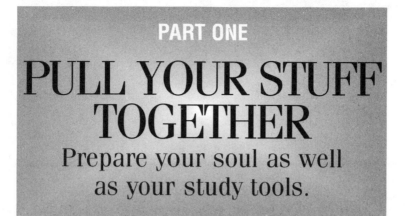

PART ONE

PULL YOUR STUFF TOGETHER

Prepare your soul as well
as your study tools.

Open-Heart Bible Study

Studying God's Word begins with attitude instead of aptitude.
JEAN FLEMING

What intangibles of the spirit and heart do we need for Bible study? If I chose one verse to capsulate the essential attitudes for approaching God's Word, Isaiah 66:2 would get my vote: "This is the one I esteem: he who is humble and contrite in spirit, and trembles at my word." We don't hear much about sticking a humble, contrite spirit and a good solid tremble in with our Bible study tools, but without them we'll shuffle around the edges of truth and never penetrate the heart of God's riches.

Let's look at three essential attitudes and why they are important for studying the Scriptures.

Beginning with a Humble Spirit
First, we need a humble spirit. A humble spirit grows in a proper understanding of who God is and who we are in relationship to Him.

God looks for a particular spirit as we approach His Word—precisely because *it is* His Word. The Bible is communication from the high and lofty One, the One who lives forever, whose name is holy, but who lives with the person of a humble and contrite spirit (Isaiah 57:15). This Word is the most complete revelation given by the God who is eternal, divine, holy, and personal. God has "exalted above all things [His] name and [His] word" (Psalm 138:2). God gives His Word a place of highest honor.

When we grasp the reality that we're actually studying God's Word, we realize that we cannot come to this Book on an equal footing with it. The human mind cannot fully fathom the thoughts, the character, the person of God.

Jack and May, a vibrant Australian couple, came to Christ in middle age. As new believers unfamiliar with the Bible, they wanted to start Bible study "at the beginning and at the bottom." They bought and read a Bible written for children before progressing to an adult Bible. At conversion they got their first good look at who they were and, more importantly, who God is. Seeing themselves in their sinfulness and God in His pristine holiness left them little confidence in their abilities to understand the thoughts of God. They began where babes start.

Like Jack and May, Gail also came to the Scriptures with childlike humility. When I met Gail I was impressed by her spiritual depth and insight. I wanted to know her story and what kind of spiritual help she had received. To my surprise, her tale included ignorance, frustration, perseverance, and finally blessing.

Gail's first attempt at Bible study ended in tears; she couldn't answer the questions. The doors of comprehension were bolted. The windows were boarded over. Not a shred of light seeped in. She read and reread but her effort yielded nothing. She wondered, *Why could a more-than-reasonably intelligent woman not understand even one question?* Thankfully, her hunger and frustration drove her to call out to God, with weeping: "Lord, please help me to understand!" The next morning she tried again. This time the door gave way; the windows of her soul let in the light; the Book came alive.

> Biblical truth isn't discovered; it is revealed, interpreted, explained, and taught by the Holy Spirit.

Jack, May, and Gail are not models of humble spirits because they were ignorant and admitted it, but because they read with humility, aware that they can't approach this Book as God's equals in intellect, character, or experience.

Gail's story can also serve as a parable. God withheld from a bright woman the ability to understand the Bible so He might implant a deeper lesson into her life. God can open or close this Book to us. An intelligent, inquiring mind is not enough. While most people do not find the Bible a completely closed book, Gail's experience illustrates a spiritual truth. Even scholars remain in the outer courts, handling the outside of spiritual things, unless God admits them into the holy of holies.

God calls us to emulate this spirit of humility and hunger, whether we are accomplished students or new converts. Intelligent, diligent, careful study is important, but the Bible doesn't relinquish its bounty to high IQs and polished exploratory skills alone. While it is true that the Bible is in many ways like any other book, it is absolutely unique. This Book reveals "God's secret wisdom, a wisdom that has been hidden and that God destined for our glory before time began" (1 Corinthians 2:7). Wisdom that no eye has seen "but God has revealed it to us by his Spirit" (1 Corinthians 2:10).

Biblical truth isn't discovered; it is revealed, interpreted, explained, and taught by the Holy Spirit. The Spirit of God alone knows the thoughts of God (1 Corinthians 2:11), and He communicates "spiritual truths in spiritual words" (2:13) to the human spirit. The language He uses is not Greek, Hebrew, or English; it is spirit. The Holy Spirit whispers it to humble spirits. So like the psalmist, let us cry out, "Let me understand the teaching of your precepts" (Psalm 119:27). Charles Simeon (1758–1836), an English preacher who taught others how to preach, wrote, "The more lowly we are in our own eyes, the richer communications we shall receive from Him."[1]

The Blessing of a Contrite Spirit

We're also to approach Scripture with a contrite spirit. A contrite spirit has an acute awareness of its failings. This awareness is accompanied by deep distress, but also gratitude that there is refuge in the mercy and grace of God.

A concordance defines contrite as "smitten, maimed, dejected." It only follows that if we picture our fallen humanity compared to God's holy splendor, we will be bruised by the contrast. As Isaiah lamented after seeing the Lord in His glory, "Woe to me!" (Isaiah 6:5). But, of course, the glory of the Gospels is that the "bruised reed he will not break" (Isaiah 42:3). Jesus doesn't break those bent with contrition. Rather, He blesses those who are poor in spirit and mourn over their sin (Matthew 5:3-4). "The LORD is close to the brokenhearted and saves those who are crushed in spirit" (Psalm 34:18).

The Word lovingly bruises as well as blesses us. If we come to the Word as self-sufficient, self-satisfied consumers of blessing, the blessing cannot penetrate the armor of self. The Word of God must pierce our thick skins, must strike stinging blows at times, must put our hips out of joint, must hold a mirror before our faces that we might see what our sin does to us. The Word must wound before it binds up. Otherwise, far worse sores fester out of sight, waiting to erupt and destroy us. A contrite spirit welcomes God's work that reveals who we really are. It limps to the throne of grace to receive the healing balm.

It is clear that God values a contrite spirit, but do we? A mature believer in the Sunday school class I attend confessed her failure to share the gospel with family members on a recent trip. She felt unfaithful and asked us to pray for her. Her words bruised me. Like her, I often lack the courage to speak the message God has entrusted to me. I was ready to stand and say so. But before I could, the class rallied to erase her discomfort. With the kindest intentions, they assured her that God had used the time and that contrition was unnecessary, even out of the question.

Just as I became aware of my sin when I heard her confession, my heart is made sensitive by the Scriptures as I read about God's plans, commands, and promises. But I must be alert to the tendency to undermine or dismiss the response of contrition. Instead of acting as devoted servants, this tendency makes us discriminating "partakers," straining out anything unpalatable to us.

Apart from the Holy Spirit's enlightening ministry to our spirits, we accept or reject God's thoughts according to our reasoning. We cart along baggage to Bible study, though we're barely aware of it. John R. W. Stott wrote, "It is essential to give up the illusion that we come to the biblical text as innocent, objective, impartial, culture-free investigators, for we are nothing of the kind."[2]

> A contrite spirit welcomes God's work that reveals who we really are.

We must face our defects—and acknowledge that we have barely begun to face them. We must acknowledge our biases and blindness—and know that we are still blind to them. We must come as open-minded and openhearted as we can—with the full realization that we are entangled in the sticky web of our humanity. And we must grieve. This is contrition.

Trembling at His Word

God wants us to come to the Bible as those who tremble at His Word. That means we need to take God seriously and believe that the Lord is who He says He is, that He thinks and acts just as He says. Trembling at His Word is the equivalent to the "fear God" used so often throughout the Scriptures.

Years ago on an Okinawan beach, my husband and some of his friends spent the day reading passages from the Gospels that took place by the water. The day climaxed with a fish and bread dinner on the shore after they read about Jesus feeding the multitudes. As they ate, my husband noticed a man watching them from the cliffs above. Roger climbed up to talk with the man and to invite him to join them. The man turned out to be a young marine involved in Satan worship. As they talked, Roger thought of Jesus' encounter with the demoniac (Mark 5:15) that they had read earlier in the day. Roger extended his New Testament toward the marine. The man began to tremble violently and ran off.

This is not the trembling that God honors; nevertheless, his trembling puts me to shame. James 2:19 says, "Even the demons believe . . . and shudder." It seems the demons in him grasped more fully than I do that this Book is alive, powerful, and dangerous. "For the word of God is living and active. Sharper than any double-edged sword, it penetrates even to dividing soul and spirit, joints and marrow; it judges the thoughts and attitudes of the heart" (Hebrews 4:12). The Bible brings me into direct contact with the clear-eyed gaze of Jesus Christ. As the demons know, this Word is not something to be trifled with or taken for granted.

Josiah was the kind of "trembler" God esteems. During his reign the long-neglected Book of the Law was found in the temple. When Josiah heard the message of the book and realized the extent of the nation's disobedience and the judgment that would surely fall on them, he tore his clothes and wept in anguish (2 Kings 22–23). Josiah approached the scrolls with a prior commitment to obey them with all his heart and soul. He reinstituted celebration of the Passover and began a vigorous campaign to rid the land of false gods. His responsiveness characterizes the man or woman who takes God's Word seriously.

A trembling heart prepares our spirits for greater intimacy with God's Word. As a teenager, E. Stanley Jones, a Methodist missionary to India for fifty years, would press his lips to passages that spoke to his heart. Jones' holy kiss seems to express the same spirit the writer of Psalm 119 recorded: "I rejoice in following your statutes as one rejoices in great riches" (verse 14), "Your statutes are my delight" (verse 24), "How sweet are your words to my taste" (verse 103), "My heart trembles at your word" (verse 161).

> A trembling heart prepares our spirits for greater intimacy with God's Word.

When we take God's Word seriously, our hands hover over the Bible in anticipation. God said His Word is the

14

necessary bread that will satisfy (Isaiah 55:1-3, Matthew 4:4). It is like snow and rain that falls from heavenly realms for a purpose. God's Word comes to nourish and refresh, to make fruitful and effective. The Bible is not ineffectual; we can expect something to happen when we receive God's message to us (Isaiah 55:10-11).

A spirit of anticipation banishes a blasé approach to Scripture. A trembling heart does not tolerate the thought that it is okay for "mature" believers past the first flushed excitement of life in Christ to stifle their yawns.

So before you open your Bible, stop! Reflect. Kneel. Pray. This book is spirit, and you need the indwelling Spirit working in your spirit to receive spiritual truth. The Author of this book is your Interpreter. Who else knows the deep things of God except the Spirit of God? He will read to your spirit the language of your Father. The translation you need is something more than Greek or English. The Spirit works both to bruise and soften your spirit, then to unfold the mysteries of God to you when you can receive them. Be alert to your spirit because it is a Book interpreted Spirit to spirit.

Jean Fleming is an author and Navigator staff member from Colorado Springs, Colorado.

2

Which Bible's Best for You?

Choose a version and format that meet your study needs.
JAMES RODGERS

As a pastor people often ask me, "Which Bible is the best one available?" The promotional literature for different translations and formats describes the merits of each, and often includes quotes and endorsements from well-known Christian leaders. Though the abundance of choices can be confusing, it is possible to find the right Bible for you by reducing the process to two basic issues. First, select the translation you want to read. Second, choose a format.

Choosing a Bible Version

To select the best Bible for your needs, you can compare the differences among the various translations or versions. The Scriptures were originally written in Hebrew (most of the Old Testament), Aramaic (a few parts of the Old Testament), and Greek (the New Testament). The vast differences between these biblical languages and English have produced three theories of translation: formal/literal equivalence, dynamic equivalence, and free translation. In their book *How to Read the Bible for All Its Worth*, scholars Gordon Fee and Douglas Stuart define these translation theories.[3]

■ **Formal/Literal.** "The attempt to translate by keeping as close as possible to the exact words and phrasing in the original language. . . . A literal translation will keep the historical distance intact at all points."[4] Historical distance means the specific terms for weights, measures, money, and idiomatic phrases are retained even though they are not a part of contemporary English.

> Though the abundance of choices can be confusing, it is possible to find the right Bible for you.

■ **Dynamic Equivalent.** "The attempt to translate words, idioms, and grammatical constructions of the original language into precise equivalents in [our] language. Such a translation keeps historical distance on all historical and most factual matters, but 'updates' matters of language, grammar, and style."[5]

■ **Free Translation.** "The attempt to translate the ideas from one language to another, with less concern about using the exact words of the original. A free translation, sometimes also called a paraphrase, tries to eliminate as much of the historical distance as possible."[6]

Each translation method is represented by a number of popular versions. The *King James Version, New King James Version, Revised Standard Version,* and *New American Standard Bible* are all literal translations. The *New International Version, New Revised Standard Version, New Living Translation, New Century Version, Revised English Bible, New Jerusalem Bible,* and the *Good News Bible* (also known as *Today's English Version*) are dynamic equivalent translations. Finally, *The Living Bible, Phillips' The New Testament in Modern English,* and *The Message* are free translations. While the versions using each approach have broad similarities, specific versions vary in wording within each category.

Each approach to Bible translation has its strengths and weaknesses. Generally, the more free the translation, the easier it will read because of the contemporary language. However, the likelihood of incorporating an idea not present in the mind of the original writer increases. Literal translations tend to be more wooden in style, but are beneficial for specific word studies because of their attention to formal accuracy. However, literal translation can also render a text more difficult to read and make understanding the message more ambiguous. Dynamic equivalence translations try to incorporate the best of both the free and the literal approaches.

It's interesting to note that when the New Testament writers quoted or alluded to the Old Testament, they used some form of translation because they wrote in Greek, not Hebrew. Sometimes they translated the Hebrew text themselves, but usually they quoted the Septuagint, the Greek translation of the Old Testament used during New Testament times. The translation work of the Septuagint produced great variety. Some parts of the Septuagint are wooden and formal, while others are free and actually include material not present in the Hebrew text. This is the work most often used when New Testament authors quoted the Old Testament.

Selecting a Workable Format

Once you've chosen a version, you can focus on the formats available for each translation. The amount of personal study you'll do will determine what features you need.

■ **Study Tools.** Most study Bibles offer a number of features to help you understand the biblical texts better. Two basic tools include study notes and cross-referencing systems.

Many Bibles contain study notes within the text or at the bottom of each page. You'll want to compare the amount and nature of these notes. Do they have a good combination of explanation and application? Both are necessary to obey God's Word. In addition, you can evaluate the introductions to each Bible book, which discuss issues such as author, date, recipients, theology, and important or challenging passages.

Cross-references list other passages related to the text you're reading. They may be found along the outside columns of the text or between the columns of text. Most cross-reference systems enable you to find verses quoted by that book's author. Some Bibles also include topical systems for cross-referencing. These Bibles have a separate reference section in the back that lists other passages about a certain subject, such as anger. If you want to do comparative study on different topics, you could consider a study Bible that includes a topical reference system.

■ **Concordances.** Many Bibles also contain a concordance. A concordance is an alphabetical index of the principle words found in the biblical text and the passages in which they're located. Concordances enable you to find familiar passages for which you don't know the reference. If you know one or two words in a particular verse, you can look up those words in a concordance and find the reference. Concordances are also helpful for topical studies. Even if you use a separate exhaustive concordance, it's helpful to have primary references included in your Bible.

■ **Maps.** The events of the Bible occurred in real places in the context of real cultural situations. Maps can help you develop a better geographic understanding of biblical lands. Usually they are included within the text or located at the back of the Bible.

■ **Readership.** A number of Bible formats target a specific group of readers, such as men, women, seniors, or teens. These Bibles often incorporate devotionals to help the targeted readership understand and apply the Bible to its unique needs.

■ **Size.** If you simply want a Bible to read, you probably don't need study tools that make it larger and bulkier. However, even many smaller Bibles include limited study features such as center-column cross-references, a few maps, and a limited concordance.

■ **Readability.** Unfortunately, the enhanced reference materials included with many Bibles have resulted in smaller print. Scan a couple of pages to evaluate how readable the text is for you. A growing number of study Bibles are available in large-print formats. Consider also whether the extra features interfere with readability. Study notes, cross-references, and testimonials can actually make the Bible less readable if they are poorly integrated into the text. Make sure that the format is not overly distracting.

> Once you've selected a Bible, the most important thing is to regularly read, study, pray, and meditate over its truths.

■ **Red-Letter Editions.** People who considered Christ's words more inspired originally developed the practice of putting His words in red. While we know that "all Scripture is God-breathed" (2 Timothy 3:16), highlighting Christ's words in red can be helpful to pinpoint the flow of the gospel passages at a glance.

■ **Other Features.** Cover composition and indexing are other features to consider. Bibles are published with leather, hardbound, or softbound covers. Leather and imitation leather covers generally last longer and wear better than their hard or softbound cousins. They are also more expensive. If you know this Bible will be your primary study source for many years, a leather cover may be worth the investment.

In addition, indexed Bibles have recessed tabs with the names of Bible books printed on them. These tabs make it easy to look up any book in the Bible quickly.

Once you've selected a Bible, the most important thing is to regularly read, study, pray, and meditate over its truths. God has given us Scripture to guide our lives, and it will direct, change, and delight us.

James Rodgers is senior pastor of Grace Bible Church in Washington, Illinois.

3

The Great
Reference Book Hunt

Simplify and enjoy collecting Bible study resources.
JOHN R. KOHLENBERGER III

"Do you understand what you are reading?"

All of us at one time or another have identified with the Ethiopian eunuch. When Philip asked him if he understood what Isaiah had written he replied, "How can I unless someone explains it to me?" (Acts 8:31). But while the Ethiopian had Philip to explain Isaiah to him, most of us go it alone in our Bible study.

Or do we?

We may not have a gifted Bible teacher at our disposal, but we do have access to many scholars' research and knowledge in books published about the Bible. In fact, so many biblical reference books are accessible, we face a different problem. How do we decide which of the thousands of available titles are the most useful in our personal Bible study? And which ones will be worth our time to purchase and use regularly?

Begin with the Best

The most important book in your biblical reference library is the Bible itself. And the best way to study your Bible is to read it, read it, read it! But unless your Bible uses words that you are familiar with, you will be as exasperated as the Ethiopian. What can you do when you do not understand the language of your Bible?

The translators of the *King James Version* (KJV) said, "Variety of translation is profitable for finding out the sense of the scripture." Ironically, this principle is especially important when you read the translation they produced nearly four centuries ago! For example, Genesis 25:29 in the KJV begins, "And Jacob sod pottage." We all know "and." Most of us know "Jacob." But who knows what it means to "sod pottage"? By consulting a modern translation, such as the *New International Version* (NIV) or the *New American Standard Bible* (NASB), we discover that to "sod pottage" means to "cook stew."

Other difficult words in this chapter also become clearer in comparative study. Genesis 25:27 describes Esau as a "cunning hunter" and Jacob as "plain." We normally use "cunning" to describe someone who is sneaky and underhanded and "plain" to describe someone who is ordinary or homely. But modern translations tell us that Esau was a "skillful hunter" and that Jacob was a "quiet" or "peaceful" man.

Even if you are strongly attached to one translation of the Bible for reading, study, and memorization, "variety of translation is profitable for finding out the sense of the scripture." I strongly recommend that you regularly consult three or four modern versions to aid your understanding and to deepen your insight. Parallel Bibles, which offer several translations of the same text side by side, can be very helpful.

The Overlooked Dictionary

The most overlooked book for Bible study is the English dictionary. The *Funk and Wagnall's Standard Desk Dictionary* not only explains the English words of my Bible, it often gives a theological definition for terms such as "baptize," "grace," and "salvation." An English dictionary can offer you a hand when comparative study falls short.

As we read on in Genesis 25, Esau sells his birthright for Jacob's lentil stew. What is a birthright? We get no help from the ten best-selling versions, because they all use this same word in translation. But my dictionary tells me that a birthright is a "privilege or possession that one is entitled to by birth."[7] Esau, as the firstborn, was entitled to some privilege or possession that Jacob wanted—and got.

If this is enough of a definition, you can read on. However, if you want to know more about the privilege or possession a birthright involved in biblical times, you can consult a more specialized dictionary: a Bible dictionary or expository dictionary. Bible dictionaries give biblical, historical, archeological, and theological information about biblical people, places, customs, and events. Expository dictionaries do word studies on any kind of biblical term; they make some of the richness of the original language available to English readers.

> The most important book in your biblical reference library is the Bible itself.

The *New Bible Dictionary,* for example, in its article on "firstborn" states, "The accompanying privileges were highly valued, and in the OT included a larger inheritance, a special paternal blessing, family leadership and an honoured place at mealtimes."[8] Lawrence Richards' *Expository Dictionary of Bible Words*, in its article on "birthright" adds, "That birthright was far more than the material possessions of their father Isaac: it was first and foremost the promise of God, the covenant oath given to Abraham and passed down from generation to generation."[9] No wonder Jacob wanted the birthright!

Bible dictionaries and encyclopedias are also extremely useful in studying backgrounds, events, and people of the Bible. To dig deeper into the background of Genesis 25, we could study hunting, foods, oaths, and covenants. By looking up their names, we could find biographical sketches of Jacob, Esau, Isaac, and Rebekah.

Study Bible Bits and Pieces

The Bible is not simply a collection of words, it is the true story of God's gracious interaction with human history, so we must also read the Bible as history. To do this, we study the lifestyle, customs, and culture of Bible people. We can learn what they thought, how they communicated, where they traveled, what they valued, how they worshiped. We can discover when and how biblical history interacted with world history, and how each influenced the other. To do this thoroughly is the labor of many lifetimes, but again much valuable information resides in quality reference books.

> Never let the use of a commentary substitute for your own personal Bible reading and first-hand research.

Study Bibles give us bits and pieces of biblical reference books for more thorough research. For example, *The NIV Study Bible* provides at the beginning of each book an introduction to the background, author, date, and message of the book. For Genesis, we are told, "The narrative frequently concentrates on the life of a later son in preference to the firstborn,"[10] and that our story of Jacob receiving Esau's birthright is one of six million other episodes in the book. Each book is outlined in detail to show its major divisions, structure, and contents.

As you read a study Bible, notes at the bottom of each page will help you better understand the text. For example, in Genesis 25:33, Jacob insists that Esau swear by an oath to give him his birthright. The note explains, "A verbal oath was all that was required to make the transaction legal."[11] Beside the biblical text are cross-references that lead us to other significant verses containing similar words and concepts. Here we find there are references to birthright in Genesis 27:36; Deuteronomy 21:16-17; 1 Chronicles 5:1-2; and Hebrews 12:16.

Most study Bibles also contain maps that trace movements and locations in biblical history. On page 53 of *The NIV Study Bible* there is a map devoted specifically to the travels of Jacob as he flees Esau's murderous wrath in Genesis 27–32.

A study Bible can be a self-contained library for basic Bible study. But if you do not want to invest in another Bible just to get its reference materials, you can find similar features arranged in biblical order in a Bible handbook.

Ways to Find Words

One of the best ways to study biblical words, concepts, and people is to look up and study every reference that relates to them. The best books for this type of Bible study are topical Bibles and concordances.

A concordance usually lists every occurrence of a particular word in the Bible. Concordances are limited to the words and spellings of a specific translation. If you use the *King James Version*, you need a KJV concordance such as *Strong's*, *Young's*, or *Cruden's*. The same is true for any other version.

However, looking up "birthright" in the KJV or NASB concordance, there are ten references. In the NIV concordance, we find only six. That is one of the problems of using only a concordance for word studies: different translations use different words so concordances will proffer different references. This is especially noticeable in the KJV with the word "faith." In the Old Testament of the KJV, the word "faith" appears only two times—yet Hebrews 11 lists eighteen Old Testament characters who lived by faith!

> Only you can decide which of the many good options are best for your specific needs.

So how can we find references to concepts shared by translations that use different words? That is where the topical Bible proves useful. A topical Bible is not limited to single words and translations. It can also discuss synonyms, phrases, and examples of biblical words and concepts. *Nave's Compact Topical Bible*, for example, summarizes four key concepts about birthright, citing eleven biblical references. It also lists five people in the Bible who forfeited their birthright, with nine additional references. Using both a concordance and a topical Bible, we can more thoroughly study biblical words, concepts, and people.

Comments on Commentaries

A commentary is the most convenient resource for Bible study because it presents the end result of scholarly research in a concise form and in biblical order. But if you consult only the end result for its convenient answers, you do not learn how to study for yourself. In addition, the commentary may not have the answers you need.

Once you have taken time to read the text, to compare translations, to define and study key words, and to dig into the background, you have answered questions and drawn conclusions. By comparing your notes with a handful of commentaries, you can verify that your conclusions are orthodox, fill in some of the blanks in your personal research, and answer some of the questions your own study could not.

I recommend eventually collecting three or four one-volume commentaries or sets to use together—much as you would use more than one translation of the Bible for comparison and contrast. But never let the use of a commentary substitute for your own personal Bible reading and firsthand research.

Building from the Bible Out

Chances are, you won't be able to buy all of these reference books immediately. So where do you begin?

Once you've chosen a few translations for comparative reading, and a study Bible based on your primary version, I recommend the following core of key resources, in order of priority:

- Good English dictionary
- Bible handbook (if your Bible does not have adequate introductions and notes)

- Bible dictionary or encyclopedia
- Topical Bible
- Concordance

If you already own an English dictionary, you can purchase this "core library" for as little as $60 in paperback. After you obtain these study aids, you may want to add an expository dictionary for more insights into the biblical languages, and a collection of Bible commentaries for comparative research.

You will discover that many different titles are available in each category of reference book. Only you can decide which of the many good options are best for your specific needs. Go to a bookstore or a church or seminary library, and take time to browse and sample these books in order to make the best decision.

As you build your own reference library, you will decide the level at which you want to enter and the level you want to reach. You are limited only by your desire, stamina, and of course, monetary resources. But knowing how to choose the right book for the right purpose will make every cent you invest in your library pay off. Your deepening understanding of God's Word enables you to understand the Lord in new ways and to worship Him better.

John R. Kohlenberger III has written numerous biblical reference books, including *The NIV Complete Concordance* and *Books About the Book: A Guide to Biblical Reference Books*. He is an instructor of Bible and biblical language at Multnomah School of the Bible in Portland, Oregon.

PART TWO

BEGIN WITH THE BASICS
Build a foundation of reliable study formats.

As Easy as ABC

Use this basic outline to delve into biblical passages.
THE NAVIGATOR BIBLE STUDIES HANDBOOK

To begin an ABC Bible study, select the passage of Scripture you will study. It should not be more than one chapter—preferably it should be a section of a chapter. Here's what to do:

1. Read the passage a minimum of three times.
2. Read it again and jot down your thoughts in a rough draft.
3. Organize your study under the following five sections, each identified by a letter of the alphabet.

A. Create a Summary Title

You may want to write your title after you have finished the rest of your study. In choosing a title, jot down two or three titles that come to mind as you study; then either select the best one from this list or form a new one from a combination of your suggestions. The title should fit the chapter or passage and be as complete as possible. The title should clearly identify the passage's content. Don't be concerned about being clever or catchy. The title can be as short as two words or as long as ten.

B. Identify the Best Verse or Basic Passage

Decide whether you are choosing a best verse or a basic passage. Write the reference of the verse or verses under the section title.

The best verse is a single reference that seems most outstanding to you as you read the passage or chapter—it does not have to include the central theme. The basic passage is a group of verses (no more than three) that includes the central message or is the key to the contents of the passage. You may want to write out the entire verse to memorize it.

> Remember to depend on the Holy Spirit, who ultimately enables us to grow in Christ.

C. Look for a Personal Challenge

As you work through the passage or chapter, ask God to challenge you in a personal way from some portion of what you are studying. Your purpose now is to accept this challenge and apply its truth in a definite way to your life. It may be something that God wants you to do or stop doing, or an attitude to develop or stop. A habit may need to be formed or broken. You may need to incorporate some truth into your thinking.

Under the heading "Challenge," begin with the number of the verse or verses from which you are taking your challenge. First, state in your own words the truth of the verse. Then tell how the challenge applies to you—what needs it reveals in your life, what shortcomings, transgressions, or neglects it indicates, or what new appreciation or understanding it opens up to you. Since the challenge is personal, use the pronouns "I," "me," "my," and "mine" in your writing.

> This ABC look at Scripture will not only help you understand the Bible, but apply it to your life.

Next, state clearly what you plan to do about it. Tell what specific action you will take to correct the weakness, to build the needed quality into your life, or to increase your understanding of this truth. Choose something practical you can do during the following week, instead of something long-term. Remember to depend on the Holy Spirit, who ultimately enables us to grow in Christ.

D. Pinpoint the Difficulties

Consider each verse in your study passage. Does it speak of anything you could not explain to another person? If so, under the heading "Difficulties" write down the number of the verse and the question or problem it raises in your mind. State the specific difficulty it presents to you.

If a difficulty can be answered by a little research (such as looking up a word in a dictionary), do the research and record the answer.

E. Describe the Passage's Essence

In the last section of your study, you may choose to summarize or outline the passage under the heading "Essence." In either case, you should record only what the passage says, not what it means. Rather than interpreting it, simply put in your own words what the Scripture actually says.

The summary is a brief condensation of the passage. Summarize all parts of the passage equally, not giving too much space to one part and slighting another. One way to do this is to write one sentence in your rough draft for each successive thought in the passage, using your own words instead of the words of the text. Then condense your summary into fewer words, combining your sentences and making them shorter. You should aim for an average of two to eight words per verse.

An outline divides the passage into its natural paragraphs and gives a brief title or heading to each section. Write down the verses included in each section.

List as many subpoints under each of the main headings as you need to define its content. As in the summary, include all parts of the passage in good proportion.

This ABC look at Scripture will not only help you understand the Bible, but apply it to your life.

The ABC Bible Study method is adapted from *The Navigator Bible Studies Handbook* (NavPress, 1979). Used with permission.

What's the Purpose?

Uncover Scripture's intent with the Timothy method.
KEVIN GREEN

As a young believer I simply read through the Bible, hoping that something would stand out to me. This approach was hit-or-miss. So was my growth. I also relied on devotional books that explained and applied the Bible for me. But this left me more dependent on the teaching of a person than on the Holy Spirit. In seminary I learned technical methods of studying God's Word in depth. But these methods were burdensome to apply to my daily walk with Jesus.

Frustrated one morning over my devotional life, I asked a simple question: "What is the Bible for?" God's direct answer changed my devotional life forever. The Lord brought to mind the definitive verse on the purpose of Scripture in 2 Timothy 3:16: "All Scripture is God-breathed and is useful for teaching, rebuking, correcting and training in righteousness." In addition, He opened my eyes to a simple yet powerful way to apply this verse to my personal Bible study. Asking key questions about the four purposes of Scripture—teaching the truth, rebuking sin, correcting spiritual deficiencies, and training in righteousness—can effectively guide us as we evaluate and apply Scripture.

> Asking key questions about the four purposes of Scripture can effectively guide us as we evaluate and apply Scripture.

Teaching the Truth

Begin with the first purpose of Scripture listed in 2 Timothy 3:16, teaching. Ask yourself, "What does this passage teach?" Boil it down to a simple statement (or statements) of truth. To help crystallize what is taught, ask these clarifying questions:

- What does this passage say about God?
- What does it say about people?
- What does it say about my relationship with God and others?

Everything in God's Word relates to these simple questions.
Jesus declared that the entire Bible hangs on the two commands to love God

and love others (see Matthew 22:34-40). Scripture becomes incredibly practical when you look at it in the light of these questions. To help cement the truths you find, write down everything you discover. Writing out your thoughts will do wonders to clarify your understanding of God's Word.

Rebuking Our Sin

The second purpose of God's Word that Paul describes is rebuke. Scripture rebukes us by revealing our sin and the ways we fall short of God's standards. Once you see what a passage teaches, prayerfully ask if there is any way that you are violating this truth. Ask:

- Am I falling short in this area? If so, how?
- If you sense conviction, ask yourself, "Where and how is this sin taking place?"

It's critical to identify clearly how you fall short. For example, it's not enough to know that you have a problem with anger. Responding properly to rebuke means specifically confessing where sin is rearing its head. Don't just say, "I have a problem with anger." Instead, identify how you sinfully express that anger: "When I'm angry, I tend to be critical of my spouse."

Next, ask yourself:

- Is this sin the problem or just a symptom of a deeper issue?

Many times, sin manifests itself in our lives as a response to other, less visible problems. Criticizing my spouse may be the result of my frustration at work or some other cause. Unless we deal with the root, the weeds will grow again. Real change demands that we go below the surface.

Correcting Spiritual Deficiencies

The third purpose of the Bible is correction. The Word of God not only rebukes us when we get off track, but it shows us the on-ramp back to the right road. Correction begins by asking, "What is the opposite of my sin?"

> The Word of God not only rebukes us when we get off track, but it shows us the on-ramp back to the right road.

For example, if I have a problem with uncontrolled anger, God desires patience and self-control. Next, ask yourself, "What action do I need to take to get back on track?" Write down specific ways that you could display the right behavior. For example, I will listen to my wife's point of view before I respond, and I will respond with a calm tone of voice. Pray that God would enable you to begin to make changes you've recognized are necessary.

Training in Righteousness

God's Word trains us in righteousness. The goal of the Christian race is to finish well. We not only get back on the right track, but we stay there. Hebrews 12:1 instructs us to "throw off everything that hinders and the sin that so easily entangles, and . . . run with perseverance the race marked out for us." The Word of God trains us to run with perseverance.

Finally, ask yourself, "What do I need to do to stay on track?" The answer may be revealed in the passage you're studying. However, you may also need to consider other Scriptures to answer this question. Maybe you need to commit to pray about the issue at hand or memorize certain verses on the subject. Long-term change demands that we transform our minds and hearts. Use this final question as a catalyst to help you develop a plan of action.

Kevin Green is the pastor of Cornerstone Community Baptist Church in Brodheadsville, Pennsylvania.

One at a Time

Summarize chapters for their unique spiritual lessons.
RICK WARREN

The chapter summary method of Bible study helps you gain a general understanding of a chapter of the Bible. In this method you read a chapter at least five times, ask a series of content questions, and summarize the central thoughts of the passage.

This is a popular method for those new to Bible study because chapters are usually fairly short, and it does not require intensive study. It can be quickly taught to a new Christian or to anyone who is interested in doing meaningful Bible study.

Ten Summary Steps
After you have selected a chapter for study, read it through at least five times. You might want to read it in several different translations.

As you reread the chapter, begin looking for the following ten specific things and write down your answers.

STEP ONE: CAPTION
Give the chapter a short, descriptive title. The shorter the title the more likely you will remember it. Try to find the key word of the chapter and fit it into your title. For example, 1 Corinthians 13 could simply be titled "Love," or Hebrews 11 might be "Heroes of the Faith." A short title will help you remember the chapter's content.

STEP TWO: CONTENTS
Describe, summarize, paraphrase, outline, or make a list of the major points in a chapter. The method you choose will depend on the literary style of the chapter and on your own preference. Some people like to summarize; others like to outline. Choose the method that feels most comfortable and one that is easy for you to do. Don't try to interpret the chapter yet, just make observations on its content.

STEP THREE: CHIEF PEOPLE
List the most important people in the chapter. Ask questions such as:

- Who are the main characters in this chapter?
- Why are they included?
- What is significant about them?

If the chapter contains pronouns (he, she, they, etc.), you may have to refer to the previous chapter to identify the people. Write down your reasons for choosing certain people.

STEP FOUR: CHOICE VERSE
Choose a verse that summarizes the whole chapter or one that speaks to you personally. In some chapters you may find a key verse that summarizes the writer's argument; in other chapters there may not be a key verse. You may want to pick a verse from which you will be writing your application, a verse you believe God wants you to apply to your life.

STEP FIVE: CRUCIAL WORDS
Write down the key word or words of the chapter. Many times the key word will be the one that is used most frequently. In some cases—such as "count" in Romans 6—the crucial word may be the most important word but not the most used one. Also, remember that a chapter may have more than one crucial word.

STEP SIX: CHALLENGES
List any difficulties you may have with the passage. Are there any statements you do not understand? Is there any problem or question you would like to study further? For instance, a certain word may catch your attention. Later you may want to do an in-depth word study on it. A question about a doctrinal matter might motivate you to do a topical study on that particular teaching.

> Choose the method that feels most comfortable and one that is easy for you to do.

STEP SEVEN: CROSS-REFERENCES
Using the cross-references in your study Bible, look up other verses that help clarify what the chapter is talking about. Ask the question: What else in the Bible helps me understand this chapter? Cross-references are important because they are helpful tools in interpreting the meaning of a chapter. They enable you to see what the Bible as a whole has to say on any teaching.

STEP EIGHT: CHRIST SEEN
The entire Bible is a revelation of the Person of Jesus Christ. In fact, Jesus used the Old Testament to teach His disciples about Himself. As you study each chap-

ter, be alert for statements that tell you something about Jesus Christ, the Holy Spirit, or God the Father. Ask yourself:

- What can I learn about the nature of Jesus from this chapter?
- What attributes of God in Christ are illustrated here?

This step may be difficult to complete in some portions of the Bible, particularly in Old Testament narratives and in passages where symbolism is used.

> The entire Bible is a revelation of the Person of Jesus Christ.

STEP NINE: CENTRAL LESSON(S)

Write down the major principles, insights, and lessons you learned from this chapter. Ask yourself:

- Why does God want this passage in the Bible?
- What does He want to teach me from this chapter?
- What is the central thought the writer is trying to develop?

STEP TEN: CONCLUSION

This is the application portion of your study. Here you should ask yourself two questions:

- How do these truths apply to me personally?
- What, specifically, am I going to do about them?

Then begin to follow through on the answers.

Rick Warren is the founding pastor of Saddleback Valley Community Church in Mission Viejo, California.

This chapter was excerpted from Rick Warren's book *Personal Bible Study Methods* (published by The Encouraging Word, 1981). This and many other resources from Rick Warren are available through the website www.pastors.com. Copyright Rick Warren. Used by permission.

God Is in the Details

Systematically analyze a passage with a verse-by-verse plan.
RICK WARREN

When you want to work systematically through a passage or chapter of the Bible, one of the best systems is the verse-by-verse analysis Bible study method.

This type of Bible study involves examining a passage of Scripture in detail by asking questions, finding cross-references, and paraphrasing each verse. You then record a personal application for each verse that you study.

Five Verse-by-Verse Steps
This study is built around a verse-by-verse analysis chart. You will follow five simple procedures for each verse that you study. To begin, select the passage you want to analyze. Work through the passage in a logical order, writing out your verse in the first space of column one, second verse in the second space, and so forth.

STEP ONE: PARAPHRASE THE VERSE
Write out the verse in your own words. Do not use one of the modern paraphrases except to get the idea of how to do it. Stay true to the verse you are paraphrasing, and try to condense rather than expand it.

STEP TWO: LIST QUESTIONS, ANSWERS, OBSERVATIONS
List any questions you have on the verse or on words, phrases, persons, topics, or doctrines in that verse. Write down any answers you are able to find (in other Bible passages, in reference books, etc.). Also record any observations you have on that verse. Mark these as follows:

Let your imagination go and be as creative as you can.

- Q = Question
- A = Answer
- O = Observations

STEP THREE: CROSS-REFERENCE THE VERSE

Using the cross-references in your study Bible or from your personal Scripture memory, write down some cross-references (try for a minimum of one) for the verse you are studying. Identify the word or phrase in each verse that you are cross-referencing. Use a concordance if you do not have a cross-referenced Bible.

STEP FOUR: RECORD CREATIVE INSIGHTS

Having thought through the words, phrases, and concepts in the verse, record insights that you get from it. These could be further observations, words, and names that you have looked up and defined, or any other thought that comes to you. Let your imagination go and be as creative as you can.

STEP FIVE: DETERMINE PERSONAL APPLICATION

Write down a brief personal application. Because of the number of verses you will be studying, you will not be able to design an application project for each verse. Instead, just try to record some devotional thoughts that come to you from each verse. Later you can pick one of the thoughts and plan to work on it. Or, if a particular verse seems to meet an immediate need, go ahead and write out an application that is possible, practical, personal, and measurable.

> Try to record some devotional thoughts from each verse.

Filling Out the Chart

To create a verse-by-verse study chart, draw six columns on a sheet of paper. Label them: Verses, Personal Paraphrase, Questions and Answers, Cross-References, Insights, and Personal Application. When you have picked the number of verses you will study, write each one in a separate space in column one, using your favorite translation of the Bible. Stick with the same translation throughout your study.

Next, fill in the rest of the columns as described in the five steps above. Refer to the sample on page 43 for ideas on how to do it.

Rick Warren is the founding pastor of Saddleback Valley Community Church in Mission Viejo, California.

This chapter was excerpted from Rick Warren's book *Personal Bible Study Methods* (published by The Encouraging Word, 1981). This and many other resources from Rick Warren are available through the website www.pastors.com. Copyright Rick Warren. Used by permission.

Verse-by-Verse Analysis Form   Book or Topic: 1 Timothy

Verses	Personal Paraphrase	Questions and Answers	Cross-References	Insights	Personal Applications
1:1 Paul, an apostle of Christ Jesus by the command of God our Savior and of Christ Jesus our hope,	Paul, one sent forth as Christ's representative, by the commandment of God, the One who saves us, and Christ Jesus our hope,	Q. What does the word *apostle* mean? A. The Greek word *apostolos* comes from the verb *apostello,* "send forth." Q. Why is God the Father, rather than Christ, called Savior?	Apostle: 2 Cor. 1:1 God my Savior: Lk. 1:47 Titus 1:3 Christ our hope: Col. 1:27	1. The name Paul comes from the Latin name *Paulus,* which means "little." 2. The name Timothy means "he who honors God." 3. Paul did not need to tell Timothy that he was an apostle, so perhaps this letter was intended to be 'read by others as well.	I must begin to see myself in the role of Christ's ambassador who has been authorized and sent out with a divine message. The authority of my witness will only be as effective as my awareness of my mission.
1:2 To Timothy, my true son in the faith: Grace, mercy and peace from God the Father and Christ Jesus our Lord.	To Timothy, my true child in the Christian faith. May love, mercy, and peace from God the Father and Christ Jesus our Lord be yours.	Q. Does the name Timothy have any special meaning? A. Timothy means "he who honors God."	My child: 2 Tim. 1:2 Christ Jesus: 1 Tim. 1:15	1. *Messiah* in Hebrew means *Christo* in Greek, which means Christ in English. Christ means "the anointed one of God."	May my name become synonymous with a life that is honoring to God, like Timothy's.

What's in a Word?

Discover what biblical writers and languages really meant.
KENT R. WILSON

"The finest words in the world are only vain sounds, if you cannot comprehend them," wrote French author Anatole France.[12] Words, even in Scripture, can be "sweeter than honey to my mouth" (Psalm 119:103), or they can be "things that are hard to understand, which ignorant and unstable people distort" (2 Peter 3:16).

Though words are the simplest of building blocks for language and communication, they can be perplexing with their myriad shades of meaning and usage. For example, in the *Oxford English Dictionary* the word "round" supports over seventy distinctly different meanings. Yet a deeper look at Scripture eventually involves the study of words and their variant meanings.

Consequently, the basic purpose for a word study is to discover the most appropriate meaning of a particular word and to understand how that meaning affects a passage as a whole. The encouraging part about doing word studies is this: they can be as elementary or as involved as the Bible student desires. Word studies can be as simple as following three easy steps with only a Bible in hand. Or they can be as complicated as a lexical and etymological study using original languages and Greek or Hebrew reference works. You decide the complexity needed based on the resources you have available, the time at hand, and the nature of the word itself.

There are only three basic steps in every form of a word study. The depth to which these steps are carried out determines the complexity of the study.

Step One: Determine Meanings and Uses
Decide what word to study by looking for key words within the passage or words whose meanings are unknown or confusing to you. Imagine you are studying Ephesians 1:7: "In him we have redemption through his blood, the forgiveness of sins, in accordance with the riches of God's grace." You could do word studies on "redemption," "forgiveness," "sin," or "grace."

In this step you try to find other possible meanings of the selected word. It may be used differently in other parts of the passage or the Bible. Or you can refer to dictionaries, concordances, or other resources for differing meanings of the word. A Bible dictionary would tell you that the word "forgiveness" from the Ephesians verse actually means "to send away" and is pictured in the Old Testament by the scapegoat. There the sins of the people are confessed on the head of a goat, which is then sent into the wilderness, never to be seen again.

A good general resource for conducting word studies is W. E. Vine's *Expository Dictionary of New Testament Words,* or the *Expository Dictionary of Bible Words* by Lawrence Richards. Both are inexpensive resources based on the English text, yet give Greek and cultural information that is understandable to anyone.

> A deeper look at Scripture eventually involves the study of words and their variant meanings.

Step Two: Discover the Best Definition

In studying a specific word only one meaning may arise. That makes your job easy. But if a number of possible definitions surface, then you decide which meaning best fits the particular passage and context. Try each potential definition within the passage.

- Which meaning best fits and is consistent with the context?
- Which meaning is compatible with other passages of Scripture?

In Ephesians 1:7, redemption can either mean "to release from something," such as in freeing a prisoner, or more specifically "to free by paying a ransom." When the word is associated with the shed blood of Christ, "ransom" becomes the best meaning since Christ's blood is the payment made for our captivity in sin.

Step Three: State the Passage's Meaning

Word studies are useful only when the word is studied in the context and illuminates the meaning of a selected passage. When the word's specific definition is applied to the passage, the meaning of the passage can be determined. Only then can one apply the passage to his or her life.

For example, the word "round" has numerous meanings until it is used in a discussion about guns, such as when someone says, "I took the round out of the chamber for safety." In step three the best definition of the word becomes the basis for interpreting the meaning of the entire passage or context.

Types of Word Studies

The three steps above can be applied to various forms of word studies depending on the resources available and the complexity of the word. Here are six different forms of word studies that use the same basic steps but different resources.

- **English Definition Study.** By using an English dictionary, various meanings of a word can be written out. Good dictionaries will also indicate word origins and foreign-language uses.
- **Origin or Etymology Study.** Here you'll need a good Bible dictionary like

Vine's or a lexicon such as *A Greek-English Lexicon* by Arndt and Gingrich to learn if the word originally derives from several words combined together. For example, "steward" is a compound word made from the word for "house" and the verb "to arrange." When Paul refers to elders as stewards in Titus 1:7 (NASB), he no doubt refers to their arranging or care of the house of God, the church. Another example: One Greek word for "worship" literally means "to kiss towards," while the Hebrew word means "to bend the knee."

> However you choose to study a word, you'll be blessed by the way its specific meaning applies to your life.

■ **Usage Study.** Here a good concordance is all you need to look for how the word is used in other passages. Study every occurrence of the word, looking for other possible meanings or patterns. You may find that James uses the same word for "trial" two times in James 1, each with a different meaning. Or that some words are unique to Paul's letters, such as "predestinate."

■ **Lexical Study.** Instead of trying to discover the various meanings of a word on your own, let a good Bible dictionary or lexicon do the work for you. In them you'll find information about the word's origin, history, meanings, and theology. Look up the word, briefly list its basic idea and meanings, then try to pick the best meaning for the passage before looking at the recommendation in the resource.

■ **Synonym Study.** Most words have synonyms whose meanings are distinct from the chosen word yet illuminating in their differences. Again, a source like *Vine's* or *Synonyms of the New Testament* by Richard Trench is helpful for finding synonyms. List each synonym with its distinctive meaning. Then evaluate the insight learned from knowing that the author chose that specific word instead of one of its synonyms.

Paul chose his words carefully in Ephesians 4:26 when he spoke about how long anger should last. He used the word for "anger" that means a more settled or long-term feeling that, if left unchecked, can sometimes lead to revenge or sin. He purposely did not use its synonym "wrath," which refers to a sudden outburst of emotion that is usually short-lived. However, in verse 31 he uses both words when he cautions against all forms of anger and bitterness.

■ **Translation Study.** Each translation of the Bible can be a resource to understand word meanings. Look up your chosen word in a number of different translations and paraphrases and you will be able to gain insight into possible word meanings and a preferred rendering. Be sure to use a combination of translation types: literal translations such as the *King James Version* or the *New American Standard Bible;* modern translations such as the *New International Version* or *New Century Version;* specialty Bibles like *The Amplified Bible;* and even paraphrases such as *The Message* or *The Living Bible.*

However you choose to study a word, you'll be blessed by the way its specific meaning applies to your life.

Kent R. Wilson is the publisher for NavPress in Colorado Springs, Colorado.

Going in Circles

Cluster your thoughts and word definitions for deeper insights.
TIM SANFORD

The goal of any Bible study is for the truth and power of God's Word to change our lives. In addition to a formal study of the Scriptures, we can do some old-fashioned soul-searching along the way.

The word-cluster method, when used in addition to a word or topical study, can accomplish three tasks. First, it will help you generate a personal, expanded definition of the word or topic. Second, it represents your personal and historical relationship with the word. Third, it can help you identify any "unofficial" definitions of the word you may have. These definitions often go unchallenged, in spite of the fact that they color your perception of Scripture and life.

> What ends up on paper should be equal to what you are thinking. Easier said than done!

A word-cluster opens up your heart, as study opens up the Scriptures. Here is how it works.

Choosing a Starter Word
Select a word to do your cluster with before you begin your in-depth Bible study. This way you get a better understanding of your "real" thinking without being biased by the "right answer." You will need to be vulnerable and honest as you do this exercise.

- If you are doing a word study, you already have your starter word. A variation is to select a word that seems the opposite of the word you intend to study.
- If you are doing a topical study, there are key words that permeate the topic. Select one or two of these as starter words.

Making Boxes, Lines, Circles
Now you are ready to begin the cluster method.

1. Write the starter word in the center of your page and draw a box around it. Turn off your internal censors, editors, and judgments. What ends up on paper should be equal to what you are thinking. Easier said than done!

2. What is the first word or phrase that comes to mind about the starter word? Write it down close to the starter word and circle it. Draw a line connecting it to your starter word. What does this second word cause you to think of? Write it down, circle it, and connect it to the previous word. This is called a thought-line. It may follow a straight line or it may look like a tree branching out all over the page. The form is not important. Continue this way until you can go no further.

3. Go back to your starter word and begin this process again. Add a new thought-line of words that occur spontaneously. You can go back to previous thought-lines or individual words at any time and add to them. Your page will look like a web of thought-lines. Feel free to put thoughts wherever they seem to fit. Don't overanalyze; just jot them down. There will be time to check for accuracy later.

> Try a word-cluster with your next study project. Let it move you from studying to soul-searching.

4. Take your time. Do not force words or thoughts, but allow enough time for thoughts to develop. You will know you are finished when you fill the page or you run out of ideas. I usually go a minimum of fifteen minutes before I consider myself finished.

Looking It Over

Once you have completed your word-cluster, take time to sit back and survey your handiwork.

1. Ask yourself questions such as:

- Do any patterns emerge?
- Do any comments surprise me?
- Are there comments or words that seem to be missing from my paper (e.g., emotion words)? Why?
- What observations can I make from this exercise?
- What life experiences play a part in the thoughts represented on my paper?

2. Write a personalized definition of the word. Pull it directly from your word-cluster (not from a dictionary). Write it down, even if it's not the definition you expected.

3. Put away your paper after you have asked all the questions and have written down your own definition. You will come back to it later.

4. Now proceed with your Bible study word as you normally would.

Opening Up Your Heart

After you have completed your Bible study of the word or topic, pull out your word-cluster paper and set it beside your study notes.

1. Ask God to speak to you about this subject.

2. Compare the study notes with your word-cluster paper. Make some observations.

- Are there some marked differences?
- Are there some blind spots?
- Are there thoughts that match up?
- Is what you say you believe actually the same as what your word-cluster reveals?
- How can your personal definition of the word better match the scriptural meaning?

By using traditional Bible study methods and the word-cluster method, you gain an understanding of the scriptural meaning of the word, plus a concrete way of discovering what you actually believe. You observe where your beliefs match up with Scripture, and you expose areas where they may not.

Try a word-cluster with your next study project. Let it move you from studying to soul-searching.

Tim Sanford is a licensed professional counselor in private practice. Tim also teaches adult Sunday school at his church in Colorado Springs, Colorado, and volunteers with Children's Hope Chest, an organization that works with orphanages in Russia.

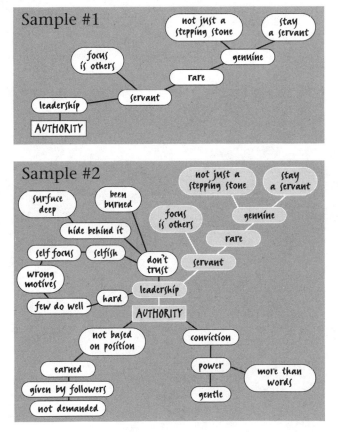

Sample #1

not just a stepping stone — stay a servant — genuine — rare — focus is others — servant — leadership — AUTHORITY

Sample #2

surface deep — been burned — not just a stepping stone — stay a servant — genuine — focus is others — rare — hide behind it — self focus — selfish — don't trust — servant — wrong motives — leadership — few do well — hard — AUTHORITY — not based on position — conviction — earned — power — more than words — given by followers — gentle — not demanded

10

Making Your Mark

Color-code a typed manuscript to pull apart a passage.
SUE KLINE

In a manuscript study you begin by turning the Bible passage you want to study into a . . . manuscript! Manuscript study is for you if:

- you are looking for a fresh way to engage with a book of the Bible;
- you love discerning patterns in Scripture;
- you have a passion for colored markers.

Before you begin, type the biblical text double- or triple-spaced, with huge margins, without any verse markings, chapter designations, paragraphs, or notes. If you have Bible software, this first step is a quick one. I, however, have enjoyed typing out the books I want to study (as long as they are short ones). In the typing process alone, I begin to view familiar books with fresh eyes.

You will also want to decide in the beginning how much time to give to this study. When I did a manuscript study of 2 Timothy with a small group, we took two weeks to complete it. The first week focused on observations we'd made and questions the text had raised. During our second meeting, we talked about any answers we'd found to our earlier questions, then shared significant lessons and personal applications.

I've also used manuscript studies for personal study. I always do short books, and it generally takes me at least a month, dividing the various steps of the study over three to four hours each week.

Walk Through the Manuscript

Let me walk you through the steps of a manuscript study using 2 Timothy as an example.

1. I read the entire text through three or four times, usually over a period of a few days. Perhaps by the second reading I'll start marking repeated words and phrases or other elements that stand out to me.

2. By the third reading, my manuscript is alive with color as I note themes, commands, key phrases, and so on. I could never bear to mark my Bible with total abandon, but when doing a manuscript study, I can let loose. I used the following for the 2 Timothy passage:

- green circles for repetitive words, such as "grace," "ashamed," and "endure"
- blue double-underscores to note one of the underlying themes—things we have in Christ, such as faith and love, grace and salvation
- purple boxes to note another theme—our partnership with God in ministry
- yellow circles to note Paul's warnings—against fear, false teaching, the flesh, and fatigue
- red circles to note references to the power and usefulness of God's Word
- black circles for commands, such as "Fan into flame the gift of God," or "Do not be ashamed to testify," or "Present yourself to God as one approved"
- orange boxes for descriptions of Paul's character and lifestyle—for example, he was a finisher, he wasn't ashamed of the gospel, he endured suffering, and he lived with purpose
- orange double-underscores to note words Paul used to describe himself—"apostle," "servant," "herald," "teacher"
- a highlighter to mark what I believed were key verses—or verses I wanted to memorize later

> Feel free to use colors, boxes, arrows, etc., in whatever way works for you. Also, different books will yield different treasures.

These techniques are examples only. Feel free to use colors, boxes, arrows, etc., in whatever way works for you. Also, different books will yield different treasures. Other features to note are comparisons and contrasts, cause and effect statements (look for "If . . . then" or "Therefore"), key people, and statements of purpose.

3. Now I read through the text again and make notes. This time I will:

- jot down cross-references that come to mind.
- write in the margin any observations. For example, where Paul wrote, "I am not ashamed, because I know whom I have believed," I noted in the margin: "Paul's fearlessness isn't the result of confidence in himself but, rather, confidence in Christ. The cure for Timothy's spirit of timidity— and mine—is a focus on my all-powerful Savior."
- look up the definitions of any words that are new to me or unclear.
- draw arrows to connect related ideas.
- write in the margin any questions I have. For example, I wanted to know who Jannes and Jambres were—Paul spoke of them as opposing Moses. Later, I found the answer in Exodus 7:11—they were Pharaoh's magicians. I might also ask of a certain sentence, "What does this mean?" I tackle those questions in step four.

4. At this stage, I like to read a commentary or check a few reference books for background information on the book—for example, the cultural and historical setting. I purposely leave the commentaries and references alone until this point. I don't want them to replace my personal study, but I have found that they can greatly enhance it once I've already gleaned what I can. I write in the margins any insights I gain from this research. I also look for and record any answers to my "What does this mean?" questions.

5. I also found it helpful to imagine myself writing the passage and to decide where I would put the paragraph breaks. Sometimes we are so locked into chapter and verse divisions that we miss the crucial flow of thought from the end of one chapter to the beginning of another. This process can reveal a flow and relationship of ideas and principles that I've missed in the past.

6. In the end, personal change is the purpose of all this coloring and "arrowing" and underlining. My final question becomes, "Lord, how do You want me to respond to this passage?" I might know the answer, having spent days, weeks, maybe months, on the study. I might need to let the study roll around in my head and heart for a few more days in order to really discern what God is saying to me. Once I know, I write it down. Then I tell a friend what God has shown me—that's for accountability. My application may require a change in behavior. It may require taking a step of faith—such as inviting my neighbor to church. Perhaps God will tell me, "Write a letter to so-and-so and encourage her, as Paul did Timothy."

> There is something about all that hands-on involvement with the text that deeply impresses it on your brain and in your heart.

Both Versatile and Valuable

As I mentioned in the beginning, I've used manuscript studies for personal insights and also in small groups. I've loved discovering the creative ways in which my small-group friends have marked their manuscripts. No two studies are ever alike.

One helpful hint for using this method in small groups: Number the lines on each page. Because you are working without chapter and verse numbers, you'll need some way to direct each other within the text. Numbering each line accomplishes this.

I've done a lot of Bible studies in the past twenty years. The books of the Bible that I know most thoroughly and personally are those I've studied using the manuscript method. There is something about all that hands-on involvement with the text that deeply impresses it on your brain and in your heart.

Sue Kline is the editor of *Discipleship Journal* and still hasn't outgrown her fascination with colored markers.

11

Let's Get Topical

Select a topic and pursue its use throughout Scripture.
THE NAVIGATOR BIBLE STUDIES HANDBOOK

A topical study is your opportunity to study directly from the Scriptures a topic that interests you. You will come out with your own personalized set of conclusions—and even convictions—on the subject, complete with application to your own needs.

The first step in a topical study, obviously, is to choose a good, manageable topic. Your topic for study may be one you have long wanted to research. It may have come up as a side issue during another type of study. Or perhaps you heard a sermon that started you thinking on the subject. You may be discipling someone who has asked you searching questions on a matter of importance to him, and you need some answers.

If you select a topic that is quite broad, such as "love," you could divide it into several studies, such as The Love of God, Man's Love for God, Love of Neighbor, or The Nature of Love.

Select the Scripture Passages

Once you have selected your topic, pick the ten to twelve best passages—those that give you real insights into the topic. Use scratch paper as you jot down possible portions of Scripture and decide which are the best. Some passages you will select will be a single verse, others a paragraph, or maybe a whole chapter.

> You will have put limits around your study and won't wander endlessly through the Bible searching for one more tidbit of truth.

A topical Bible, concordance, or computer Bible concordance will help you find the passages relating to your topic. Look up related words as well as the main one. (If your topic is salvation, for example, look up such words as "forgiveness," "redemption," "born again," "atonement," and "eternal life.")

Jot down the references of those portions where your topic is treated. If your Bible has a subject index, you might find some references on your topic listed there.

This process of selecting the best passages will take some time as you look up and compare various Scriptures. Be patient; once you have chosen your best passages, you will have put limits around your study and won't wander endlessly through the Bible searching for one more tidbit of truth.

Once you have your passages, list the ten to twelve references with a key thought beside each one for quick identification.

Summarize or Outline the Passage

The Scriptures you have chosen and listed form the basis for the rest of your topical study. Summarize separately the content of each passage. Then read through the summaries one or more times, noting the main points the passages teach and how they fit together.

On another sheet of paper write a summary of your summaries, condensing, rearranging, and combining where possible. This should be a composite statement of what the Scripture teaches on the topic. Or you may prefer to state the truths you have discovered in outline form, once you have written your summaries. When you have rewritten the summary or outline to your satisfaction, copy it in final form in your study notebook.

Find a Key or Favorite Verse

As you read through each of the Scripture passages for study, find one that seems to contain the kernel of what the Bible teaches on this topic. Or if you prefer, simply choose the verse you like best on the topic. Record it under the heading "Key Verse" or "Favorite Verse." You may want to memorize this verse as a reminder of the topic.

Think of Topic Illustrations

Your Scripture passages for study, as well as your summary or outline, may contain some illustrations of the topic. If so, list them by reference under the heading "Illustrations." For example, in a study on faith you might use Abraham as an illustration, listing Hebrews 11:8-10.

You may also think of other illustrations from the Bible, from your own life, from nature, or from the experiences of others that you could add here.

Write an Action Application

> A vast number of possibilities exist for carrying out the applications you make.

Review the parts of your study and go back over each of the Scripture passages, asking God to show you some aspect of the truth that you should apply in your life.

First, write a brief statement of the truth contained in the verse or verses you select for your application. Then add a brief statement of the need or condition in your life, in your relationship to the Lord, or in your relationship to others, that should be changed or improved according to the truth you have learned or about which you have been reminded.

Finally, record a simple plan of action you will follow to help bring about the needed correction or build the quality into your life. This might be spending time in prayer about the need, memorizing a verse of Scripture, making restitution to someone, doing some kindness, or scheduling a special project. A vast number of possibilities exist for carrying out the applications you make. This is the cream of your study and should always be exciting—though not always easy—as you see God work in your life according to His promise.

The Topical Bible Study method is adapted from *The Navigator Bible Studies Handbook* (NavPress, 1979, 1994). Used with permission.

PART THREE

KEEP IT INTERESTING

Add depth and variety
to Bible study times.

Something Old, Something New

Unearth fresh and vital truths from Genesis to Malachi.
BARBARA J. PATRIQUIN

An Old Testament book study allows you to glean applicable lessons from the experiences of the Israelites, ordinary people like us, as they encountered God. In the study you will trace two aspects: God's character and principles to live by.

If your time is limited, however, you can study one of these aspects and leave the other for another time. However you approach the Old Testament, you can find something old (what you already knew) and something new (fresh insights) in its pages. Here are the steps to follow:

Step One: Pick a Book
Pick an Old Testament book to study. One of the more action-packed books filled with events would be the best place to start. Plan to read the book through in segments, taking one to three chapters at a time.

Step Two: Make a Chart
Make a chart with divisions for Chapter and Verse, Events, God's Character, Principles to Live By, and Application.

> What can you see about the nature of God—His heart, mind, and will?

Step Three: List the Events
List the events and their references as you read about them. You may not want to write down every little situation, but rather the more detailed ones. For example, from Joshua 1:1-9 you might include the following: God commissioned Joshua to go in place of Moses to take possession of the Promised Land. With the commission was the promise of His presence and that He would give them the land. God told Joshua to keep the law and meditate on it always, as a means of success.

Step Four: Identify Character Traits
List the character traits of God—qualities He displayed about Himself in each encounter with people. What can you see about the nature of God—His heart, mind, and will? For example, again from Joshua 1:1-9, God makes promises, He

gives specific instructions, He expects obedience, and He understands our fears and addresses them.

Step Five: Trace the Principles

Trace the principles or truths that can be learned from transactions between God and His people. A principle, according to Webster's dictionary, is "a fundamental truth, or motivating force upon which others are based; a rule of right conduct." A principle to live by can be supported as God's truth throughout the Scriptures.

Here we are tracing principles or truths upon which God wants us to pattern our lives. For example, when God speaks to us we must listen and act upon what He says as truth. God always means what He says. God's Word is our road map; we are to follow it and cling to it for success in life. As we act on His Word, God's promises will go with us and be our confidence.

Step Six: Write Applications

As you relate what you are reading to your personal life, the Holy Spirit may speak to you about some specific circumstances in your life where this Scripture applies. Jot it down with the intent to do something in response to God's leading. Another time you may just see general ways of relating the passage to your life. List these, too. The purpose of this step is to take note of what God is trying to tell you.

> A principle to live by can be supported as God's truth throughout the Scriptures.

Step Seven: Summarize the Comments

When you have completed the entire book in this manner, review your findings. Reread your comments on the character of God and summarize them. Write down the most prevalent attributes of God that you traced throughout the book. Then review the principles you discovered.

- Which ones were reinforced most often through the book?
- Which ones seem most important?

Finally, see if there are any patterns in your applications. One point may stand out above all the others, or they may be leading to one specific need in your life.

I use this Old Testament study method in my devotions and in extended times with the Lord. It has helped me get a better handle on the content of the Old Testament. The Old Testament has become relevant to my own experiences as I have seen God's character throughout its pages and related the principles to my everyday life.

Barbara J. Patriquin is a freelance writer and a homemaker.

The Treasures of Kings

Biblical rulers underscore the value of godly obedience.
NATIVITY ABECIA

A while ago I was saddened reading the biblical story of King Amaziah, who began well but then turned from the Lord (2 Chronicles 25). When I reached Uzziah's story in chapter 26, I hoped it might encourage me. But he, too, started strong and then grew tired of pleasing God.

Through weary failure stories, I pressed on. My heart swelled with joy when I read, "Jotham grew powerful because he walked steadfastly before the LORD his God" (27:6). I had been ready to give up on this book, but God had other plans.

As I dug deeper, I discovered that the stories of these kings have a lot to offer us—if we'll discard our preconceptions and really think about how they apply to our lives. On the surface many of these narratives are similar. But embedded within them are rich lessons about walking with God for a lifetime.

So grab your Bible, notebook, and pen, and get ready to unearth buried treasure from these historical books of Scripture. Here's what to do:

Step One: Record Observations

To begin, choose a king's story and read through it, listing the biographical information provided in the text. Then consider these questions:

> How are you like the king you're studying?

- What were this king's strengths and weaknesses?
- How did these traits affect his relationship with God over the long haul?
- How did he finish his reign as king?

Asa, for example, was committed to God, though his father, Abijah, had been evil. Asa expelled the temple prostitutes, got rid of the idols his father had made, and deposed his grandmother, the queen mother, because she made an Asherah pole. However, Asa failed to remove the high places dedicated to pagan gods.

Remember that many accounts in 1 and 2 Kings are repeated in 1 and 2 Chronicles. I found Asa's story in both 1 Kings 15 and 2 Chronicles 14–16.

Step Two: Compare Him to You

How are you like the king you're studying? List the character traits—good and bad—that you share with him.

I share Asa's passion to do mighty things for God. But I also share a significant weakness with him. At a critical moment Asa relied on the king of Aram instead of the Lord (2 Chronicles 16:9). Sometimes I can look to people for help before I look to God. When an emergency arrives, God can seem less powerful and real than flesh-and-blood friends.

> The Bible has recorded the failures and successes of these kings for a purpose.

Identifying common elements between their lives and ours makes it much more difficult to dismiss these men as mere failures. We see that our struggles and decisions are not that far removed from theirs.

Step Three: Write an Application

Next, write down the king's attitudes and behaviors you want to imitate and those you want to discard.

I wrote, "I want to be godly in my private devotions, just as Asa was in the early years of his reign. I will do what is right in the eyes of the Lord by putting God first. Specifically, I need to tithe and to keep the Sabbath. I also need to deal with areas of potential idolatry in my life. I think materialism and loving people more than God are two things that may be idols for me."

Step Four: Etch the Truth

Now think about ways to etch God's truth into your heart. What verse grabbed your attention? Memorize it, or write it on a piece of paper and stick it on your mirror. Or look for a song in a hymnal to sing as a response to Scripture. Be creative as you consider how to drive home what you've learned.

Step Five: Respond in Prayer

It's time to respond to what God has taught you. Ask Him to help you do what is right and avoid the wicked actions of the kings. You might want to write your prayer in a journal or notebook.

Step Six: Tell Someone

Finally, share your discoveries with someone else. I asked my prayer group to pray for the character traits I needed to develop. I also asked them to confront me gently when they see me stumbling into habits I want to discard.

The Bible has recorded the failures and successes of these kings for a purpose: to highlight the attitudes, reactions, and relationships that bring us closer to God or lead us astray. Their stories and experiences can guide us on our journey and help us walk with Jesus—the King of kings—until we see Him face to face.

Nativity Abecia lives in Baguio City, Philippines.

14

Growing Through Proverbs

The wisdom book can sharpen your character.
TERRY POWELL

The book of Proverbs is a thirty-one-chapter catalog of short, pithy statements revealing God's perspective on daily life. You'll find maxims on everything from keeping a lid on your temper to the side effects of drinking too much. Proverbs also comments extensively on relationships, mentioning more than 180 different kinds of people.

The study that follows is a systematic approach to examining Proverbs chapter by chapter. It will prompt you to look for several different kinds of content and spur you to think more deeply about the daily contexts in which they're applied.

This study also uses nine key words to help you to observe the text from different points of view. These key words serve the same purpose as a metal detector: They enable you to locate treasure that's buried just beneath the surface of the biblical soil. Let's look at each word and illustrate the process using Proverbs 15.

Key Word One: Communication
Start your devotional time with a moment of communication with the Lord. Ask Him to increase your powers of observation and to show you how the verses in the chapter relate to your life. Make the psalmist's prayer your own: "Open my eyes that I may see wonderful things in your law" (Psalm 119:18). When you finish praying, read the proverb that corresponds with the day of the month.

Key Word Two: Home
Home is one of the primary contexts in which we apply biblical truth to our lives. As you read a chapter, try to link its content to situations around the house. Does a verse make you think of your relationship with your spouse, roommate, or one of your children? Many of the passages in Proverbs could be applied to your home life. To keep from getting bogged down, look for one verse that gives insight relevant to your life at the moment.

As I read Proverbs 15, I pondered this question: Which verse speaks loudest to the things I'm currently experiencing at home? God's Spirit directed my attention to verse 1: "A gentle answer turns away wrath, but a harsh word stirs up anger." I recalled a recent incident in which I had reprimanded my two sons for arguing, using harsh words of my own. What an example! I had yelled at them for yelling at each other. I quickly saw a connection between this verse and my experience. It nudged me to confess my outburst to the Lord and to apologize to the boys.

Key Word Three: Attitudes

These key words serve the same purpose as a metal detector.

An attitude is a feeling or internal reaction we have toward a person or circumstance. Terms such as "humble," "joyous," "teachable," "pessimistic," and "thankful" describe a few attitudes. As you read each chapter of Proverbs, consider these questions:

- What attitudes does the text compliment?
- What attitudes does it censure?

These questions made me sensitive to Proverbs 15:31: "He who listens to a life-giving rebuke will be at home among the wise." This verse exalts a teachable spirit—a willingness to learn from others. The Lord reminded me of how valuable feedback can be, even if it seems painful at times. He doesn't ask me to agree with everyone, but He does expect me to listen and consider what has been said.

Key Word Four: Relationships

Relationships are one of the most common subjects in Proverbs. What connections do you see between the chapter and your relationships outside your home? Each chapter may speak to the way you relate to friends, neighbors, coworkers, and even your enemies. Does one verse prick your conscience and convict you to make specific changes in the way you're relating to someone?

When I viewed Proverbs 15 with relationships in mind, I stopped at verse 22: "Plans fail for lack of counsel, but with many advisers they succeed." I had been wrestling with a decision for days but couldn't sort through the issues to reach a satisfactory conclusion. This verse convicted me about my solo effort to make the decision and prodded me to make an appointment with a close friend to talk about it. His input clarified my alternatives and helped me work through my fuzzy thinking.

Key Word Five: Actions

Some proverbs refer to behavior patterns that God either applauds or denounces. In each chapter, try to pinpoint one behavior that God wants you to implement or curb. However, don't compile a long list of action plans from each chapter. When we try to make many changes at once, we'll likely overload our capacity and fail to make meaningful changes, resulting in frustration instead of increased obedience.

Sometimes the action we need to take will be related to one of the other observations in the study. For example, the Home phase of the study had already convicted me about speaking harshly with my boys. A few minutes later, as I meditated on the chapter in light of my actions, God reminded me again to apologize to my kids later in the day. Two steps in this study worked in tandem to move me toward one concrete action.

Key Word Six: Consequences

Other passages in Proverbs describe the positive or negative consequences of a particular course of action. They cause us to consider the ramifications of our decisions, motivating us to discard unwise behaviors.

Proverbs 15:25 warned me about the damaging consequences of pride: "The LORD tears down the proud man's house." This verse reminded me of a similar passage I had previously memorized: "Pride goes before destruction, a haughty spirit before a fall" (Proverbs 16:18). After reflecting on these verses, I thanked the Lord once again for the success of a seminar I had just led. These proverbs reminded me of how dangerous it is to accept the credit that the Lord deserves.

Key Word Seven: Tongue

Over 100 verses in Proverbs talk about the tongue. Identifying these verses will help you understand God's "philosophy of conversation." These verses describe both conversational sins and ways to minister to others with our words.

When I focused on the subject of speech, verse 23 grabbed my attention: "A man finds joy in giving an apt reply—and how good is a timely word!" Providing an apt answer or a timely word requires a listening posture. I asked the Lord to help me overcome a tendency to interrupt others during conversation.

Take as much time as you need to soak deeply in the wisdom of this practical book.

Key Word Eight: Expression

The word "expression" refers to something we voice or convey to others. We express our faith when we witness to an unbeliever, lead a Bible study, or share a truth that has impacted our lives.
As you probe the proverbs, pick out a truth to express to someone else.

- Did a verse encourage you?
- Did the Holy Spirit expose a problem that you need to discuss with a friend?
- Did something remind you of a wayward friend who needs your loving reproof?

Ask the Lord for an appropriate opportunity to express something you learned in the chapter.

Key Word Nine: Remembrance

Which maxim from the chapter challenged you the most or left the biggest impression on your conscience? Spend some time meditating on that verse and committing it to memory. Memorization gives the Holy Spirit fuel to work with throughout the day and increases the likelihood of applying biblical truth to your life. The verses you've already identified in your study are strong candidates for memorization.

Since the Lord had used Proverbs 15:1 to convict me of my rude tone of voice around the house, I decided to memorize it. Now when I'm tempted to over-react during a clash, I recall that verse's words: "A gentle answer turns away wrath, but a harsh word stirs up anger." These memorized words spur me to whisper an SOS prayer and keep me from a major blowup.

Growing in Character

The first letters of the words in this study form an acronym: CHARACTER. Applying truth from Proverbs to your life daily will stimulate character growth in your walk with God. As you use this study, remember that it is a tool to enhance your vision as you read, not a legalistic straightjacket. Think of it as a kaleidoscopic approach that enables you to see many facets of truth in each chapter.

Some days you may discover verses for each word. Other days may not yield as many observations. If necessary, take two or three days to explore a single chapter. Take as much time as you need to soak deeply in the wisdom of this practical book.

Terry Powell is a professor at Columbia International University in Columbia, South Carolina. He is the author of *Lord, Give Me Wisdom* (WinePress).

15

Tell Me That Again

An old story revives when told from a new angle.
MARSHA CROCKETT

Are you looking for new insight into a lesson you've heard since you were a toddler in Sunday school? It's easy to skip right past those dusty old passages and miss the treasures there. Or maybe the stories are new to you. Then it's easy to get distracted by the drama and action and miss God's message from the lives of the men and women.

Here's a method to dig out the hidden jewels found in familiar Bible stories. We'll use the story of David and Goliath recorded in 1 Samuel 17 for our example, but it works for any other story, too.

How to Start the Study
Concentrate on one segment of the story at a time: one character, one symbol, one event, even one word or phrase that grabs your attention, especially if the story or life spans many chapters. You may think the story of David and Goliath is one event, but there are several segments that can be studied in depth. The following list exemplifies how a story can be broken into segments.

- David's arrival and confrontation with brothers (verses 20-30)
- David and Saul's interaction (verses 31-39)
- Equipped by God (verse 40)
- David meets Goliath (verses 41-47)
- David's attack and victory (verses 48-50)
- After the victory (verses 51-58)

> It's easy to skip right past those dusty old passages and miss the treasures there.

Ask Questions About the Story
As you consider the selected story, ask these questions for further insights:

- What changes do you see in one character from the beginning of the story to the end? David started out as a naïve shepherd but then became an errand boy who argued with his brothers. Is this the same David at the end of the story? What caused him to change? How about Saul? He seemed willing to help David at first but had a change of heart. What happened?

■ What general topics or problems does this story address and what specific lessons does it teach on the subject? Much is written in Scripture about faith, but what do you learn from David's faith in particular? You can see that he used the gifts and tools he had at hand even when they appeared inadequate for the job. What about facing opposition? You learn the enemy is not always on the other side of the fence. Sometimes opposition crops up in our own camp, sometimes from well-intentioned teammates. To deepen your understanding of that segment of Scripture, study a particular phrase or topic using cross-references, a concordance, or other translations.

Find a Life-Application Symbol

Consider a symbol in the story and how it applies to your life. For instance, Saul's armor leads me to ask, "What false reinforcements do I use in my life to face tough problems? Do I trust in my own might or God's?" Or, consider the five stones. Do they demonstrate a lack of faith on David's part? Why did he need five if God was fighting for him? Perhaps it's not a matter of, "What if I fail?" but a question of, "How many stones will it take to kill a giant, and am I prepared to do the best job?"

> Ask anything and everything, and then try to dig for answers.

Ask Anything and Everything

Ask anything and everything, and then try to dig for answers. What made David different from every other Israelite man? How did God prepare David for this moment? What phrases show David's faith? Have I ever acted like David's brothers, or like Saul? How did David's mission change from the beginning of the story to the end?

Ask God to reveal His treasures to you as you study His Word. "If any of you lacks wisdom, he should ask God, who gives generously to all without finding fault, and it will be given to him" (James 1:5).

Marsha Crockett is a freelance writer and the author of *See the Wind, Mommy: Sensing God's Presence Through the Lives of Your Children* (Baker, 1996). She is active in her church's women's ministry.

16

Thickening the Plot

Role-playing a Bible narrative brings it to life.
KATRINA BAKER

Oh, my dear Hannah. I know, perhaps better than anyone else, how difficult today will be for you. Today we will take Samuel, our precious son, to Shiloh, to the tabernacle of the Lord. There we will dedicate him before the priest into the service of the Lord for all his days. I know your heart must be breaking as you dress him for the trip. His eyes are shining, full of love for his mother. And he smiles sweetly at you in trust and confidence. You return his smile, and your eyes also shine. But they shine with tears.

It has been more than three years since you've been to Shiloh. I remember that trip well. You were in such anguish. There was an emptiness in your soul, a longing for the child you could not have. I wanted to fill that need for you. I did all I could to comfort you and to encourage you. I always gave you twice as much as Peninnah at the time of the peace offering. I thought that my efforts and my gifts could ease your pain. But I should have known better.

Your faith in God amazed me then, as it does now. Even though He had closed your womb, you continued to seek Him, to ask Him, to trust Him. I remember the vow you made to God. You promised that if God would give you a son, that you would dedicate him to the Lord. But you went one step further. Our people's custom in the Nazirite vow was always to dedicate a son after a number of years. But you promised our son to God "all the days of his life." Your longing was that great, your desire was that strong.

Those paragraphs open my essay, "Elkanah's Letter," which approaches the story found in 1 Samuel 1–2 from the perspective of Elkanah, Hannah's husband. When I began working on the essay, I didn't realize how it would impact my devotional life. Rewriting a familiar story from a new viewpoint brought fresh insight and made the story personal. Instead of just knowing the story, I now felt it. It filtered through my mind, my experience, and to some extent, my imagination, and emerged as a part of me.

I hadn't changed the facts or rewritten history. I just imagined what Elkanah might have said to Hannah on the day they took Samuel to the tabernacle. I imagined that he would have looked back at all they had been through and praised Hannah for her faithfulness and attempted to comfort her sadness.

In writing this essay, I really dug into God's Word. I studied the custom behind the Nazirite vow and the meaning of the name Samuel. I read and reread the passage until I knew it inside out. I found that using this method to study the Bible boosted my sometimes dry devotional life. I found myself meditating on Scripture day and night.

If you'd like to breathe life into a biblical story, here's how you can use this method to boost your own devotional life.

> Rewriting a familiar story from a new viewpoint brought fresh insight and made the story personal.

Writing Your Essay

Obviously, the first step is to write your story. Try these guidelines to bring out the writer in you.

1. Choose your story. Pick a Bible story you would like to write about from a different perspective. Make it a familiar story: one you've heard often as a child, or one you've read many times.

2. Read through the passage at least five times to familiarize yourself with the details. If possible, read it in several different translations to get a "feel" for the story behind the words.

3. Investigate the background. If you have a good study Bible, read over the notes carefully. Or use other tools such as a Bible commentary or a Bible dictionary to dig more deeply into the story. Learn at least two new things about the characters, their situation, or the relevant customs of the time.

4. Pick your viewpoint character. Decide who will tell the story. Choose a person who was there, but someone other than the main character of the story. In my essay, I chose Hannah's husband, Elkanah. In the biblical passage, the narrator focuses primarily on Hannah. But he does describe Elkanah's great love for Hannah as well. That was my starting point.

5. Write your essay. Begin to write your story from the viewpoint of the character you've chosen. Don't worry about spelling, grammar, or punctuation. Just write. Incorporate biblical facts and the new things you've learned from your background study. You can write your essay as if it were a journal entry, a newspaper article, a letter, an obituary (if applicable), or any other form of writing. Be creative and enjoy writing it.

Some Helpful Guidelines

As you write the essay, keep these guidelines in mind:

1. Take the pressure off. You don't have to be a professional writer to do this exercise. Everyone has an imagination. Use yours!

2. Stick to the facts. The point of this method is to understand a familiar Bible story in a new, more intimate way—not to rearrange the facts to say something other than what God intended. Base your essay on the truth of God's Word.

3. Keep a flexible time limit. You can finish your essay in thirty minutes or take thirty days. You can scribble something down and come back to it in a few days to refine your work, or you can ponder the story for a week before you write anything. There is no right or wrong approach. Do whatever works for you.

> It is a great way to take a break, step back, and refresh your devotional life when you're in a slump.

With the essay completed, you will find that you know your chosen story well, perhaps better than any other, since you have used your intellect, your emotions, and your imagination to work through it. Take some time to record your insights. Thank God for the new things you've learned. And, if you're feeling brave, share your story with others.

However, I wouldn't recommend this method of Bible study for everyday use. It requires a level of study, thought, and creativity that could be draining if implemented daily. But it is a great way to take a break, step back, and refresh your devotional life when you're in a slump. Try using this method three or four times a year, or whenever you find yourself intrigued by a particular person in the Bible.

Katrina Baker is a freelance writer and stay-at-home mom in Pittsburgh, Pennsylvania.

Can't decide on a story? Try one of these:

- The story of the Flood from the perspective of Noah's wife or one of his sons (Genesis 6–8)
- The crossing of the Red Sea from the perspective of an Israelite child (Exodus 14)
- The destruction of Jericho from the perspective of Rahab (Joshua 2 and Joshua 6)
- The story of David from the perspective of a Philistine soldier (1 Samuel 17)
- The story of David, Bathsheba, and Uriah from the perspective of Bathsheba (2 Samuel 11–12)
- The resurrection of Lazarus from the perspective of Lazarus (John 11)
- The story of the Last Supper from the perspective of Judas (Luke 22)
- The story of Paul's conversion on the road to Damascus from the perspective of one of Paul's fellow travelers (Acts 9:1-9)

17

All Nature Sings

Learn more about God through His creation.
KAREN JOHNSON ZURHEIDE

It's hard to imagine a more life-related volume than the Bible. Yet sometimes we need to hear its words in fresh ways. Especially if we've been walking the road of faith for a while, a different angle can enhance our Bible reading.

A recent visit to the majestic mountains of Colorado affirmed this truth to me in an unusual way. As a New Hampshire native, love of mountains is in my blood. But I now live on the plains of Oklahoma and seldom experience mountain heights anymore. Thus, I found the impact of Colorado's peaks especially powerful.

As I admired their towering wonder, I began to think about the mountains in the Bible. Right away I recalled several prominent peaks in God's Word: Mount Sinai, Mount Zion, the Mount of Transfiguration, and the Mount of Olives. Those thoughts spurred my curiosity, and with a little effort I discovered more than a dozen mountains in the pages of the Bible.

My goal was not to learn about mountains as such, but to read and contemplate the biblical events involving them. What happened on those peaks? What might I learn by carefully studying the passages that included my favorite natural wonder?

As crazy as I am about mountains, they don't captivate everyone. But perhaps some other aspect of God's creation tugs at your heart. As a change from your usual mode of study, choose an aspect of the natural world that interests you, and examine the related biblical accounts.

■ **Are you a beach person?** Look at the stories that involve water settings, including the Nile, the Red Sea, the Jordan, the Sea of Galilee, and Paul's Mediterranean journeys.

■ **Or maybe the sky interests you.** You might want to study the heavens, the sun, the moon, the stars, creation, God's promise to Abraham, the day the sun stood still over Joshua and his army, the Day of the Lord in Joel, the wise men's star, and the black sky at Jesus' death.

■ **Are you an animal lover?** God's Word is full of animals. Begin with the Creation story, but don't overlook Noah's passengers, Balaam's donkey, Elijah's ravens, David's sheep, Daniel's lions, Jonah's worm, and Jesus' triumphal-entry donkey.

■ **If plants fascinate you,** consider the Garden of Eden, Moses' burning bush, Jonah's vine, the parable of the sower, and Jesus' vine and branches illustration.

> Perhaps some aspect of God's creation tugs at your heart.

To do this study well, you'll need some basic Bible reference tools to help you look up verses and understand them in context: a good concordance, a Bible dictionary, and a commentary if you want to do in-depth study of the passages you examine.

To illustrate how this study works, I'll describe in part my study on mountains.

Find the Nature Verses

First, identify the verses related to the element of nature you're studying. You may work from memory or use a concordance. For example, I looked up verses about the following mountains in Scripture:

- the mountains of Ararat: Genesis 8
- Abraham's mountain: Genesis 22:1-19
- Mount Sinai: Exodus 19:1-25, 24:12-18, 32:7-16
- Mount Carmel: 1 Kings 18:16-46
- Mount Moriah: 2 Chronicles 3–7
- the mountains in Psalms: Psalm 46, 121, 125
- Mount Zion: Psalm 48, 125, 133
- the mount of temptation: Matthew 4:1-11
- the mount of the sermon: Matthew 5-7
- the Mount of Transfiguration: Matthew 17:1-9
- the Mount of Olives: Matthew 24:3–25:46; 26:30-56; Luke 19:28-40
- the mount of ascension: Matthew 28:16-20; Acts 1:1-12

Develop Your Questions

Next, develop some questions to guide your inquiry into each passage of Scripture. Some of your questions should help you make basic observations on the passages you've chosen. Others might be creative application questions to help you think about how the things you've observed relate to your life. I used the following questions to look closer at the mountains in the Bible:

- What do I see about God?
- What do I see about people?
- What happened when people spent time on this mountain?
- Would I have liked being on this mountain? Why or why not?
- What can I learn about myself from this mountain?
- What meaningful new name could I give to this mountain?

Let Questions and Answers Surface

Depending on the number of passages you've selected, you might finish your study in one sitting or you might stretch it out for weeks. Each time you sit down to study the Scriptures, ask the God of nature to reveal truth you can apply to your life. Meditate imaginatively on the images in the stories, and answer each of the questions you brainstormed in the last section. Allow other questions to surface, and be prepared to think about familiar passages from a fresh perspective.

The Exploration's End

It's not essential to come up with a single application or idea that harmonizes what you've discovered. The purpose of this study is not so much to find answers as to see God's Word with new eyes. You may look at old, familiar passages differently and perhaps study some obscure ones for the first time. It's an opportunity for God's Spirit to speak to you while tailoring your exploration to a personal interest.

> May God's Spirit refresh you as you explore the Bible in new ways.

To conclude my study, however, I did consider a few summary questions:

- How has my view of mountains changed?
- My view of God?
- Of myself? While we tend to think of "mountaintop experiences" as the high points of life, the things that happened on biblical mountains were often difficult. Mountains are beautiful monuments to our Creator. They are also places where God has met people for millennia. From now on, when I experience "mountain peaks," I will do so more expectantly, seeking God and anticipating the possibility of significant change in the process.
- What lessons have these passages of Scripture brought to life? After studying so many different mountains in the Bible, one thought stands out to me: The God of those mountains is also the God of the individual. I'm even more amazed that He would want an intimate, personal relationship with me.

My Rocky Mountain high pointed me toward God and His Word. May your natural interests do the same for you. Whether you're studying alone or in a group, may God's Spirit refresh you as you explore the Bible in new ways.

Karen Johnson Zurheide is a freelance writer in Edmund, Oklahoma. She is the author of *Learning with Molly* (Spectacle Lane Press).

Reading the Bible as Literature

Enjoy the creative styles God employs in His Word.
CLINTON ARNOLD

Many Christians would describe the Bible as a God-given guidebook for life. Yet people who pick it up for the first time find it quite different from the guidebooks and manuals they usually use. The Bible doesn't provide an indexed list of instructions dealing step-by-step with the issues of life, such as "This is what you should do if . . . ," or, "Here are eight criteria for finding a good church . . . ," or, "If you have come to Christ from a background in secular humanism, this is where your worldview now needs to change."

Rather, when we thumb through the Bible's pages, we find different kinds of writings. There are numerous stories, the lyrics of dozens of songs, as well as wise sayings, personal letters, and the records of prophecies.

What kind of a guidebook, then, is this? A brilliantly conceived one! For through the various kinds of literary styles in the Bible, God has given us not only instruction, but also the story of His grand plan, inspirational examples of the faith and failure of His people through the years, songs that help us express our deepest hurts and longings to God, and much practical insight about living day to day with one's life oriented around God and His purposes.

Because there are a variety of literary styles in the Bible, we need to consider how to read each type so that we can better grasp God's word for our own situation.

The Common Narrative

The most common literary type in the Bible is narrative. A narrative is a story, an account of something that happened in the past. Most of the Old Testament consists of narrative, as seen in books like Genesis, Joshua, and 1 Samuel. In the New Testament, the Gospels and Acts are narrative texts.

In contrast to childhood stories such as *The Wizard of Oz* or *Moby-Dick,* biblical stories, or narratives, are rooted in authentic history and are vitally important for conveying truth about God and His purposes. We can be certain that when the

Bible speaks of specific people, they had a real existence in time and place.

It is important, though, not to reduce the biblical narratives to mere history. They reveal God to us. The individual narratives combine to convey the story of God at work among His people—creating them, delivering them, teaching them, warning them, fighting for them, and showering them with His love and mercy. Ultimately, we could say that the biblical narratives tell us the story of redemption. They relate how a loving God saved His people from their awful plight. Jesus Christ is the centerpiece of this plan.

Each of the individual narratives communicates still more to us. They teach us a variety of lessons about God and life. Yet in looking for these lessons we need to be careful not to read into them morals they were not intended to convey. The following guidelines should help us discover truths in narrative texts.

1. Read the whole story at least three times. A basic familiarity with the story and all of its details is crucial to interpreting correctly. In the first reading, strive to obtain a general appreciation for the story. In subsequent readings, focus on discerning some of the crucial elements of the story as outlined below.

Some biblical books, such as Genesis, are made up of a number of individual narratives. It is ideal to read the specific passage in light of the entire book.

2. Identify the plot and the principal characters. In reading any story, we naturally identify the characters and try to understand the plot. After the characters are introduced, the conflict emerges, followed by a resolution. The story of Joseph (Genesis 37–50) provides a good example of this pattern.

> We need to consider how to read each literary type so we can better grasp God's Word for our own situation.

3. Learn about the historical setting. Since each of the biblical narratives took place in history, knowing the setting and circumstances of the narrative helps us better understand the story. Let's say you are reading Luke's account of Paul's ministry in Ephesus (Acts 19). To gain a greater appreciation for the story, you will want to learn something about the city of Ephesus, the worship of the goddess Artemis, and the nature of the occultic arts in the ancient world. Bible encyclopedias and good commentaries are indispensable for this part of the task.

4. Find the moral or other lessons the story teaches. Each biblical writer purposefully selected certain episodes to narrate. That purpose often relates to conveying truth about God, His plan of redemption, and how we are to live in relationship to Him. As readers of the inspired text, we discern what the author's purpose was for writing it. What is the lesson to be learned?

For example, in John's account of the feeding of the five thousand people (John 6:1-15), he ends the narrative by referring to this spectacular event as a "miraculous sign that Jesus did." This story therefore functions as one more indicator to the readers that Jesus is indeed the Messiah, the Son of God (see John 20:31). John points out that the crowds drew their own conclusion about the nature of Jesus' Messiahship that differs markedly from what Jesus Himself was teaching (verse 15).

The narrative may also impart additional truth about God and His purposes. In drawing this out, we need to be careful not to "overinterpret" the passage. For example, it is doubtful that there is anything particularly significant in the fact that Jesus used fish and bread when He fed the five thousand, or in the number of fish and loaves (two and five), or even in the fact that it was a small boy who originally provided the food that Jesus multiplied. We can infer, however, that Jesus is concerned with our physical well-being and can miraculously provide for us. Even more significant is Jesus' declaration of Himself as "the bread of life" (John 6:35) who "comes down from heaven and gives life to the world" (verse 33). Because of this, we need to put a much higher priority on obtaining "food that endures to eternal life" (verse 27). The larger context can therefore provide important clues for interpreting both the meaning and relevance.

5. Research what the rest of Scripture teaches about the lessons. Old Testament scholar Douglas Stuart says that, "although the Old Testament narratives do not necessarily teach directly, they often illustrate what is taught directly and categorically elsewhere."[13] To check your interpretation, determine whether it finds support elsewhere in Scripture.

6. Think about how the story contributes to the book's overall theme. As we interpret each of the individual biblical narratives, we should always ask ourselves how they contribute to the overall purpose of the book. The book itself may provide a number of clues that will help us interpret the significance of parts of the respective narratives. This is particularly apparent, for example, in John's use of the word "sign" in his gospel.

The Emotions of Poetry

The book of Psalms is the most well-known collection of poetry in the Bible. Some poetic texts can be found even in narrative portions of the Bible, such as the "Song of Moses" (Exodus 15:1-18) and the "Song of Deborah" (Judges 5). Even in the New Testament we can find poetic pieces within narratives and the letters of Paul, such as Mary's song to the Lord in Luke 1:46-55 and the poem of praise magnifying the Lord Jesus Christ in Colossians 1:15-20.

To interpret poetry, we must first recognize the vital role of human emotion. The book of Psalms reveals how God's people responded to Him as they faced both threatening and joyous situations. The book consists of cries to God for help or vindication, jubilant prayers of thanksgiving to God, expressions of mourning to God over great loss, and compositions designed to lead the gathered people of God in worship.

All of these are words spoken to God by His people. However, this does not mean these poems are any less the inspired Word of God. On the contrary, they are Spirit-inspired compositions preserved to help us express ourselves to God in a variety of life experiences. As we interpret individual passages of poetry, the following principles will help to enrich our understanding:

1. Determine what type of poem it is. The 150 psalms—like other biblical poetry—represent a wide variety of poetic styles. While we normally interpret an individual passage in light of the flow of thought in a given book, we interpret the psalms individually, apart from their context. More important, we need to discern the occasion for the composition of each psalm and its specific use. This will be closely linked to the type of poem it represents. Here are a few examples of these occasions. Consult a good commentary or Bible handbook for additional help and a complete listing of the types of psalms.

- **Prayers for deliverance.** This is the most common kind of prayer in Psalms. See Psalm 22, which includes the cry, "O my Strength, come quickly to help me" (verse 19).
- **Songs of thanksgiving.** These songs give expression to the gratefulness of God's people for His help and deliverance. David begins his song of praise to God with the words, "I will exalt you, O LORD, for you lifted me out of the depths" (Psalm 30:1).
- **Hymns of praise.** These are songs of praise to our awesome God for who He is and what He has done (for example, Psalms 8, 19, 66).
- **Poems of grief.** Numerous psalms disclose the deep sense of pain and suffering experienced by God's people at times of death, loss, or serious struggle (see Psalms 39, 42, 44).
- **Calls for action.** Portions of some psalms (usually the prayers for deliverance and the poems expressing grief) record the extreme emotion of the people of God against perpetrators of evil. The language of these psalms is often exaggerated. It is vitally important to realize that these words are expressed to God with the clear conviction that He is the one who avenges evil.

2. Interpret the imagery. In contrast to the relatively straightforward descriptive language of prose, poetry employs far more metaphors (figurative language) and similes (comparisons). For instance, the word "like"—commonly used to introduce a simile—occurs 178 times in the Psalms and only twenty-six times in Genesis.

The idea of security and productivity in life is compared to "a tree planted by streams of water, which yields its fruit in season" (Psalm 1:3). The Twenty-Third Psalm elaborates on the metaphor of the Lord as a shepherd. The Lord does not literally use a rod and a staff (verse 4). These tools of the shepherd represent God's ministering and comforting presence with us.

3. Observe the literary style. Learning about common styles of Hebrew poetry will help us interpret the book of Psalms and other poetic texts in the Bible.

- **Repetition.** One feature of Hebrew poetry is repetition. Sometimes a key word may occur repeatedly in a psalm, such as the word "righteous" in Psalm 11. This gives us insight into the theme or key thought.

■ **Parallelism.** Hebrew poetry also frequently contains parallelism, a method in which one line helps to interpret another. *Synonymous parallelism* is when the second line restates the first in different words: "When Israel came out of Egypt, the house of Jacob from a people of foreign tongue" (Psalm 114:1). *Antithetic parallelism* uses two lines to form a contrast: "Blessed is the man who does not walk in the counsel of the wicked. . . . But his delight is in the law of the LORD" (Psalm 1:1-2). *Synthetic parallelism* is similar to synonymous parallelism, but the second line advances the thought of the first: "But his delight is in the law of the LORD, and on his law he meditates day and night" (Psalm 1:2).

The Words of Wisdom

Wisdom is a valuable perspective on life that informs us as we make our decisions. A truly wise person knows firsthand, by years of observation, what the consequences are to decisions people make throughout life. But biblical wisdom travels beyond this. It makes God the fountainhead of wisdom. Proverbs 1:7 says, "the fear of the LORD is the beginning of [wisdom]." According to biblical wisdom, the starting point for gaining wisdom is to orient one's life to God and seek to please and learn from Him.

The books of Proverbs and Ecclesiastes are collections of wise sayings designed to help people make responsible decisions in life. Most of the sayings are worded in concise and catchy ways to help the Hebrew people memorize them. Some of this word play is obviously lost in the translation to English. Like poetry, the proverbs normally employ parallelism and metaphors.

In applying the proverbs to our lives, we need to guard against an overliteralism on two fronts:

1. Proverbs point to the truth. The proverbs should be seen as general principles for guiding our behavior and choices. When we read in Proverbs 12:5 that "the plans of the righteous are just, but the advice of the wicked is deceitful," it does not mean that we should take advice only from Christians. A nonChristian financial planner may have some sound ideas for helping a Christian avoid undue debt and put together a good budget. In general, the proverb is

> Yet in looking for these lessons we need to be careful not to read into them morals they were not intended to convey.

better interpreted to mean that Christians need to be discerning in taking advice from nonChristians, especially as it regards ethical and spiritual matters.

2. Proverbs are not formulas. As Gordon Fee and Douglas Stuart point out, "proverbs are not legal guarantees from God." They point to particular outcomes that are likely to follow when one chooses a certain course of action. One may think of many exceptions to the saying, "If a king judges the poor with fairness, his throne will always be secure" (Proverbs 29:14). This verse certainly cannot guarantee that leaders will remain in political office as long as they act righteously and fairly (however much we wish this to be true). In principle, the proverb teaches that people will typically respect and favor a civic or political leader who acts out of principle and fairly resolves disputes and allocates resources.

The Point of Parables

Jesus was a storyteller. He would often tell a story to make a point. The gospel writers refer to His stories as parables.

Some people have misunderstood Christ's parables as elaborate allegorical mysteries about the church in which every detail had a hidden meaning. Thus, in the famous parable about the good Samaritan, some have seen the Samaritan as representing Christ, the man who fell victim as Adam, Jerusalem as the heavenly city of peace from which Adam fell, and the thieves as the Devil and his evil angels. Such an interpretation requires a fertile imagination. So what is the proper way of interpreting a parable? How do we avoid a novel interpretation never intended by our Lord?

Some Bible teachers have reacted to this extensive allegorizing and have suggested that only one point exists in any parable. They say the various details of the story only add to the color and drama of the parable. For instance, some would say that in the parable of the prodigal son, the main point is the generous forgiveness of the father. But even if that is the focal point, can't we learn anything from the attitude of the older brother?

A number of Bible teachers are now saying that a limited amount of allegorical interpretation is appropriate when interpreting the parables. Consider the following when you interpret a parable:

1. Identify the main characters. The different characters in the parable provide different points of view about the action described in the parable. In his excellent book *Interpreting the Parables,* Craig Blomberg suggests that the relevant teaching of the parable often revolves around these characters.

2. Look for contextual clues. The introduction to the parable, the context of the parable, and the historical circumstances surrounding Jesus' speaking of the parable will help in accurately grasping what the parable teaches. Jesus told a parable about a king going on a trip and leaving money to his servants to invest (Luke 19:11-27). As it turns out, some invest well and one does not; the good investors are rewarded and the poor one is punished. Luke introduces the parable, however, with the comment that Jesus told the parable "because he was near Jerusalem and the people thought that the kingdom of God was going to appear at once" (Luke 19:11). Clearly, then, one of the main points of the parable is the fact that the King (Jesus) would delay the complete establishment of His kingdom.

3. Investigate the historical details. We cannot fully appreciate the teaching of the parables until we understand certain cultural, social, political, and historical ideas of the times. Without sensing the terrible racial tension between the Samaritans and Jews, for example, the parable of the good Samaritan loses its punch. For these matters, use a good Bible encyclopedia.

4. Consider the viewpoint of each main character. While a parable may contain a number of valid points, these lessons generally stem from the perspective of each of the primary characters. For instance, in the parable of the prodigal son (Luke 15:11-32), we can derive three lessons related to each of the three characters: (1) the prodigal son teaches us about the importance of repentance, (2) the father's response to his repentant son gives us an appreciation of God's incredible love and forgiveness, and (3) the example of the older brother warns us against coldheartedness.

5. Translate the lessons into our context. The final step is to restate the lessons of the parable in ways that apply to our lives.

The Passages of Prophecy

Perhaps one of the most hotly debated areas of scriptural interpretation has centered on prophecy. Much of the debate has focused on the book of Revelation and passages throughout the Bible that speak of what is yet to come. As a result of this confusion, some Christians have tended to neglect the study of prophetic texts. They may not want to enter the dispute, or they may think that if the experts disagree, what chance do they have of figuring it out!

Nearly one-fifth of the Bible consists of prophecy. Therefore, it is important to spend some time thinking about how to properly interpret these passages. Keep the following points in mind as you interpret biblical prophecy:

1. Read the whole prophecy. One verse or passage cannot be isolated from the context of the complete prophecy. Carefully read the whole section in light of the entire book.

2. Learn the historical context. All of the prophecies were spoken to God's people at specific times and in particular situations. Most of the Old Testament prophecies relate directly to Israel's exile and return from exile. Once again, a good Bible encyclopedia will help you understand the historical setting.

3. Is the passage messianic? There are many Old Testament prophecies that point to the coming and work of the Messiah, Jesus (see Isaiah 9, 11, 52–53). A sure way to determine this is to see what prophecies are quoted or alluded to in the New Testament as fulfilled in Jesus Christ.

4. Has the passage been fulfilled? Most of the Old Testament prophecies have already been fulfilled. For instance, God has already judged Babylon, Assyria, the Philistines, Moab, Damascus, Cush, and Egypt in fulfillment of Isaiah 13–21.

5. Consider multiple fulfillments. One unique characteristic of biblical prophecy is the possibility of double or even triple fulfillments. Daniel prophesied the coming of an "abomination" that would desolate the temple (Daniel 9:27; 11:31; 12:11). This was originally fulfilled in 167 BC when the Syrian ruler Antiochus Epiphanes entered the holiest place of the temple and forced the Jews to sacrifice pigs on the altar. This prophecy was fulfilled again in events surrounding the destruction of Jerusalem in AD 70. It will be fulfilled finally in the course of events at the end of time (see Mark 13:14).

6. Discern the literal from the symbolic. This is perhaps the most difficult part of interpreting the book of Revelation. Certainly not everything can be taken literally, but much can be. No one really expects a literal eagle to rescue a pregnant woman and fly her to the desert (Revelation 12:13-17). The symbols represent another reality either in the past (from our perspective) or yet to occur in the future. We need to carefully interpret the meaning of symbols. It is doubtful that the eagle represents the United States, as someone once suggested, in spite of the fact that the eagle is our national symbol. We need to interpret the symbolism in terms of its meaning to the original readers. Because the interpretation of prophetic symbolism can be difficult, it is probably best not to espouse a given interpretation with unbending certitude.

7. Ask what you can learn. Because the primary function of prophecy was not to serve as a timetable for future events, it is important not to limit our expectations of what we may learn from its texts. For instance, try reading the book of Revelation to answer the questions: Who is Jesus? What did He come to do? You may be surprised at how much you learn.

Dr. Clinton Arnold is professor and chairman of the Department of New Testament at the Talbot School of Theology, La Mirada, California.

19

Encounters with the Savior

What would Jesus do? Review His life to find out.
CINDY HYLE BEZEK

For many of us, becoming intimate with Jesus is our highest ambition. Why is it, then, that this same worthy goal can sometimes be our biggest frustration? It just seems too hard to become personal with Someone whose face we have not seen, whose voice we have not heard, whose hand we have not touched.

Encountering Jesus in Bible study can help us know Him more intimately. A good translation of one of the Gospels (ideally, a red-letter edition) is the only tool required. However, a Bible atlas and a copy of the synoptic Gospels (a book in which the texts of Matthew, Mark, and Luke are presented side by side to show the "whole picture" of Christ's life) may add meaning to your time in the Word.

Jump into Jesus' Ministry
Select a passage from one of the Gospels. The book of Mark is a good place to start because it jumps right into Jesus' ministry. Depending on the amount of time you can spend, select either an entire chapter or a single event to study. If you have time, and if the event you choose is recorded in the other gospels, use the synoptic Gospels or your Bible's cross-references to read all versions of the incident.

1. Read the passage through once to establish the background and setting. As you read, jot down some basic information: Where is Jesus? Record the town, if mentioned, as well as the more specific location such as the synagogue, a mountaintop, or someone's home.

2. Determine the background to this event. This will help you place the Lord's words and action into context.

- Where had Jesus been just prior to this event? Using a Bible atlas to locate the various towns in which Jesus ministered helps us to better understand the astonishing distances Jesus traveled and to gain appreciation for the breadth of His ministry.
- Now examine His physical circumstances. Is He likely to be tired, hungry, sweaty?

■ Finally, consider the types of people with Jesus. Is He with a crowd, or an intimate circle of friends? Are the people Gentiles or Jews? If they are Jews, are they followers of Jesus or not? To what sect do they belong?

3. Either summarize or quote everything Jesus says. Also notice what Jesus does not say; sometimes this reveals more about Him than His words do. For example, in all three gospel accounts of Jesus casting demons out of a man (or men, as recorded in Matthew) and into a herd of pigs, the people plead with Him to leave them (Matthew 8:28-34; Mark 5:1-17; Luke 8:26-37). Nowhere is it recorded that Jesus answers them—instead, He simply gets into His boat and departs.

> Encountering Jesus in Bible study can help us know Him more intimately.

4. Note His feelings, tone, and attitude. Feelings, tone, and attitude are the indicators that help us relate to Jesus on a human level. For example, notice the situations where Jesus is amazed, angry, distressed, or compassionate. See how He gives strict orders to some people (Mark 3:12; 5:43), how He strongly warns others (Mark 1:43), and how He ignores still others (Mark 5:36).

5. Observe the ways He responds to people. Does He grant their requests? Does He answer their questions? Does He act or react to people?

6. Record what others say to Jesus, or about Him. Don't limit your observations to human dialogue, however. God, Satan, and the demons also talk to or about Jesus, and what they have to say is also important in our understanding of Him.

7. Consider their impressions of Jesus. How do people seem to feel about Jesus? Does He surprise them? Entertain them? Anger them? Who do they think He is? Where do they think He gets His power? Often these impressions are stated explicitly, but sometimes you may have to read between the lines.

8. Look for how people respond. Once you've considered their words and impressions, the next step is to look at how people respond. After their encounter with Jesus, what does Scripture say people do? Do they follow Him? Laugh at Him? Ask Him to leave? Plot to kill Him? Everyone who meets Jesus responds to Him in some way. Evaluate whether the people you are observing respond correctly. If they do not, why don't they? What would be a better response?

Your Impressions of Jesus

The last two questions guiding this study focus on application. As you address all the other issues outlined above, you find that an impression of Jesus emerges, often different from what you would have expected. Sometimes you may feel bewildered by Jesus. Other times you may be magnetically drawn to Him. You may even find yourself somewhat frustrated by some of His actions.

9. How has your impression changed? How is your new impression of Jesus different from what you used to think about Him? Pause a few moments to share your feelings about Jesus with Him.

10. How will you respond to Jesus? No one meets Jesus and remains the same. By this point in your study, a personal application may already be obvious. If not, review your notes, praying for insight as you do so. What characteristic of Jesus' life would you like to see more prominently in your own? Did the people's responses to Jesus convict or inspire you? How, specifically, can you worship, witness, or minister more effectively as a result of your encounter with Jesus? Ask yourself, "What is Jesus saying in this passage that could change my life, and how can I work with Him to make it happen?"

> Sometimes you may feel bewildered by Jesus. Other times you may be magnetically drawn to Him.

For example, after reading in Mark about Jesus putting aside His plans to listen to and care for the people who constantly interrupted Him, I realized how my own intolerance for intrusions prevented God from using me to minister to people's genuine needs. I repented of my selfish attitude and now am allowing the Lord to make me more open to the interruptions some people have wisely called "divine appointments."

Once you've committed to applying what the Holy Spirit has taught you in the passage, end your study time by praising Jesus for what you've learned from Him and for what you appreciate about Him. As you practice this Bible study method over time, you will find yourself knowing Jesus better and better.

Cindy Hyle Bezek is a freelance writer from Evansville, Indiana.

20

The Art of Asking

Consider the questions Christ posed and answered.
TODD D. CATTEAU

Jesus often asked questions as a teaching strategy. During a personal study of the Gospels, I discovered that these questions make great material for group or individual Bible study.

Most of Jesus' questions fall under one of three categories.

1. Jesus asked questions to validate His teaching. Many times Jesus asked questions to prove that what He said actually made sense. In Matthew 6:25 Jesus made the significant statement, "Do not worry about your life." To validate this teaching, He followed it with a series of questions: "Isn't life more important than food and clothes?" "Aren't you more valuable than the birds?" "Can worry add a single hour to your life?" When we honestly answer such questions, we can't help but agree with Jesus' original statement.

> Many times Jesus asked questions to prove that what He said actually made sense.

Other examples of validating questions appear in Luke 6:27-32 and 9:23-25.

2. Jesus asked questions to challenge false ideas. Jesus lived in a religious culture in which false ideas flourished—and so do we. He challenged these ideas by asking questions. In Luke 13:1-2 Jesus challenged the Jewish understanding of suffering. Any type of suffering was thought to be a direct result of sin (see John 9). Following a report of a tragedy involving some Galileans, Jesus challenged Jewish false assumptions by asking, "Do you think that these Galileans were worse sinners than all the other Galileans because they suffered this way?" (verse 2). His question forced listeners to reconsider their current views.

Other examples of challenging questions can be found in Matthew 15:1-3 and 16:13-15. Such questions confront our traditional, and sometimes wrong, views of God.

3. Jesus asked questions to deepen our faith. Often Jesus prefaced a miracle with a question, such as, "Do you want to get well?" (John 5:6). It seems like a preposterous thing to ask! Perhaps Jesus intended to help the person identify the object of his or her faith, and, in so doing, to deepen that person's faith in Him.

Jesus also asked faith-building questions after episodes that demonstrated a lack of faith. In Matthew 14:31, for example, Jesus rescued Peter from his water-walk, then asked, "Why did you doubt?" That question had to ring in Peter's ears for the rest of his life and probably helped him through difficult situations.

Working Questions into Bible Study

How can we work these questions into a Bible study?

1. Find a question. The first step is to find a question of Jesus. In the Sermon on the Mount alone Jesus asked at least a dozen. At the end of this chapter you will find twenty questions to get you started.

In a group study, you can choose one of two different routes. For a structured study, the leader can select the question to be studied, ask group members to complete the chart in advance, and compose discussion questions to bring to the study. In a more relaxed group, you may want to let members choose a question on the spot, then fill in the chart together.

> Jesus lived in a religious culture in which false ideas flourished—and so do we.

2. Identify the question. After selecting a question, determine whether it is a validating question, challenge question, or a faith question. Sometimes a question will fall into more than one category. Once you've agreed on the question type, follow the appropriate steps in the following study chart.

Validating Questions	Challenge Questions	Faith Questions
Question "What good will it be for a man if he gains the whole world, yet forfeits his soul?" (Mt. 16:26).	**Question** "And why do you break the command of God for the sake of your tradition?" (Mt. 15:3).	**Question** "Who touched me?" (Lk. 8:45).
Step 1—Find the statement being validated. "If anyone would come after me, he must deny himself and take up his cross and follow me" (Mt. 16:24).	**Step 1—Identify the false ideas being challenged.** Tradition is more binding than the law of God.	**Step 1—Determine the context of the question.** A woman suffering from bleeding reaches out to touch the edge of Jesus' cloak and is healed.
Step 2—List potential objections to the statement. This sounds painful! Why must I deny myself? What could be better than gaining the whole world?	**Step 2—Discuss the reasons for these false ideas.** Tradition provides stability. Tradition allows us to avoid difficult decisions.	**Step 2—Determine the question's significance.** Jesus has not come just to heal but to develop relationships with people of faith.
Step 3—Describe how the objections are resolved. The payoff is far greater than the sacrifice. No earthly pleasure is worth cashing in your soul.	**Step 3—Arrive at the clearer understanding.** Traditions need to be abandoned if they conflict with God's law.	**Step 3—Ask how the question deepens faith.** The woman is assured that Jesus loves her enough to seek her out. A relationship with Him is more important than healing.

Finishing with Issue-Related Prayer

After you have worked through the chart, close your study with a prayer that relates to the issues you have discussed.

- For validating questions, pray that God will enable you to see more clearly the spiritual rationale behind Jesus' teachings.
- For challenge questions, ask God to help you understand Him based on truth, not false assumptions.
- For faith questions, ask God to help your mustard-seed faith grow. Ask Him to help you recognize that only through Him can you experience abundant life.

Prayer must be an integral part of the study if we want Jesus' questions to impact our lives.

Todd D. Catteau is a pastor in Denison, Texas.

Twenty Questions from Jesus

Here are some questions to get you started. Classify each as a validating, challenge, or faith question. Some could fall into more than one category.

1. "Why do you look at the speck of sawdust . . . ?" (Matthew 7:3)
2. "Which of you, if his son asks for bread, will give him a stone?" (Matthew 7:9)
3. "Who is my mother, and who are my brothers?" (Matthew 12:48)
4. "How long shall I put up with you?" (Matthew 17:17)
5. "Which is greater: the gold, or the temple . . . ?" (Matthew 23:17)
6. "How many loaves do you have?" (Mark 8:5)
7. "Who do you say I am?" (Mark 8:29)
8. "Why do you call me good?" (Mark 10:18)
9. "Why are you bothering her?" (Mark 14:6)
10. "Why have you forsaken me?" (Mark 15:34)
11. "If you love those who love you, what credit is that to you?" (Luke 6:32)
12. "Why do you call me, 'Lord, Lord,' and do not do what I say?" (Luke 6:46)
13. "Were not all ten cleansed?" (Luke 17:17)
14. "What do you want me to do for you?" (Luke 18:41)
15. "Did not the Christ have to suffer these things . . . ?" (Luke 24:26)
16. "Will you give me a drink?" (John 4:7)
17. "You do not want to leave too, do you?" (John 6:67)
18. "Woman, where are they?" (John 8:10)
19. "Are there not twelve hours of daylight?" (John 11:9)
20. "Shall I not drink . . . ?" (John 18:11)

The Commands of Christ

Search the Gospels for the Son's directives from the Father.
PETER THEODORE, JR.

After studying parts of the Old Testament several years ago, a friend of mine remarked that he wished the New Testament would be as directive for the Christian as the Old Testament law was for the Israelite. That comment launched me on a study of the Gospels, looking for mandates from Christ.

A simple reading of the Gospels confirms that these books are not as minutely prescriptive as the Mosaic Law. At the same time, I discovered a wealth of clear commands that bring stability, direction, and fulfillment to our lives. In fact, the New Testament is emphatic about knowing and heeding Christ's commands. Keeping His commands is the strongest evidence of knowing (1 John 2:3-6), following (John 8:31), and loving Christ (John 14:15,21-24). Even more, rejecting the commands brings judgment (Matthew 7:21-23; John 12:48). The Master said, "Everyone who hears these words of mine and puts them into practice is like a wise man who built his house on the rock" (Matthew 7:24).

When I study and obey these commands, my intimacy with Jesus grows stronger as I hear Him speaking again and again to the issues of my life. I'm invigorated by knowing and obeying the expressed will of the Lord.

Recording the Commands

Do you want to study the commands? To begin, formulate a reasonable plan for reviewing each gospel. Consider the amount of time you can devote to the study, and divide the gospel(s) into manageable segments accordingly. If you're studying Jesus' commands in a small group, you may want to assign different portions of the same gospel to individuals. This will accelerate your study.

Jesus' commands can be found in any verse that declares authoritatively what must or must not be done, thought, said, or allowed. As you read the words of Christ in a chapter or section (a red-letter edition saves time), simply list each command and its reference in a separate notebook. Some people also like to highlight Jesus' commands in the text of their Bibles.

Studying the Commands

After you've recorded the commands in a chapter or section, reread the verses surrounding each one to understand the context. Then consider these questions:

- What topic(s) does the command address?
- What is the immediate context of the command?
- How did the command challenge the original audience?
- Is a commentary needed to give me more insight?
- What timeless principle(s) does this command embody?
- What is the command telling me, and how should I apply it?
- Are there related passages?

A chart that lists some or all of these questions will help focus your study. You can jot short phrases or longer notes for each command using these questions as headings. For example, in Mark 12:17 Jesus commands, "Give to Caesar what is Caesar's and to God what is God's." My study chart looked like the one on page 100.

Categorizing the Commands

> I discovered a wealth of clear commands that bring stability, direction, and fulfillment to our lives.

After you've listed the commands and studied them, group them into categories, such as warnings, belief, discipleship, humility, forgiveness, the Holy Spirit, endurance, etc. The chart lists several categories with select references.

You may also want to break some categories down into subcategories. For instance, subcategories under the topic of love might include love of God, of people, of self, of enemies, and of fellow believers. These subcategories can serve as a reference tool for further thematic study.

Applying the Study to Life

Before you finish the study, decide on an appropriate personal response to what Christ has decreed. Specifically, consider what changes in your life are necessary to obey certain commands. Here are several ways to align your life with the will of Christ as you apply His commands.

1. Pray for the Spirit to counsel, teach, and remind you to obey Christ's commands. Jesus taught that this was one of the primary roles of the Holy Spirit. "But the Counselor, the Holy Spirit, whom the Father will send in my name, will teach you all things and will remind you of everything I have said to you" (John 14:26).

2. Memorize commands that correct or encourage you. Post them in visible places in your home or vehicle so you can reflect upon them often.

3. Review your life by comparing it to each category. Are you truly pleasing God or merely deceiving yourself (Matthew 7:21-24; James 1:22-25)? What do your spouse, children, friends, neighbors, or coworkers think? Ask them!

4. Choose a command that you struggle with. Develop a specific action plan to obey it. Write down your plan and share it with a trustworthy friend who can help keep you accountable.

5. Repent and confess sin as necessary (1 John 1:9). This study will probably uncover some shortcomings. Your repentance and confession will bring spiritual healing and increase your intimacy with the Lord.

6. Evaluate your life regularly in view of the completed chart (Psalm 26:2; 139:23-24). If you clearly type the results of the study, your summary will be a better tool for ongoing spiritual inventory.

> Specifically, consider what changes in your life are necessary to obey certain commands.

Christians are rightly enamored with the promises, deeds, and love of Christ. Nevertheless, we must not neglect His commands. They, too, are expressions of His love for us. In an age that asks, "What would Jesus do?" there is no substitute for finding the answers in the directions He's already given us in His Word. As we obey them, we will find stability, fulfillment, and joy.

Peter Theodore Jr. is the pastor of family ministries at Occoquan Bible Church in Woodbridge, Virginia.

Study Chart
Mark 12:17

Reference	Command	Topic(s)	Context	Challenge to Original Audience	Timeless Principle(s)	Personal Application	Related Passage(s)
Mark 12:17	"Give to Caesar what is Caesar's and to God what is God's."	• Giving • Stewardship • Duty to God • Submission to government	Jesus is speaking to the Pharisees and Herodians, who are trying to trap Him with a tricky question about conflicting loyalties.	Jesus rebuked the Pharisees and Herodians with an unexpected answer: Paying taxes to Caesar doesn't dishonor God.	Both God and the government place demands upon me that I am obligated to honor.	I'll carefully report my nonsalary income to the IRS and willingly give God my all.	Ecclesiastes 8:1-6 Matthew 17:24-27 Romans 13:1-7 Titus 3:1 1 Peter 2:13-14

22

Amen, Amen

Study how Jesus presented the truth in His teachings.

TODD D. CATTEAU

Remember the childhood rhyme "Cross my heart, hope to die, stick a needle in my eye"? As children those words signified our absolute pledge of honesty. Other phrases such as "Swear on a stack of Bibles," and "Swear on my mother's grave," and "Scout's honor" confirmed the truthfulness and seriousness of our statements.

Jesus also used particular words as a preface to some of His statements. The words "amen, amen" are used twenty-five times in the gospel of John. This phrase has been translated a variety of ways. The *King James Bible* renders it "verily, verily." Both the *Revised Standard Version* and the *New American Standard Bible* translate the double amen as "truly, truly." Other variations include "most assuredly" (NKJV), "very truly" (NKJV), "I tell you for certain" (CEV), and "I tell you the truth" (NIV). *The Message,* though it does not translate the phrase consistently, offers many interesting paraphrased renditions: "Take it from me," "It's urgent that you get this right," "I say this with absolute confidence," "Believe me," and, "The truth is. . . ."

However this phrase is translated, when Jesus said "Amen, amen," He underlined the authority of His teaching by reminding listeners that His words were certain and reliable. He proclaimed the truth and understood that He was the embodiment of that truth. Truth matters because each of us lives according to what we believe to be true. Our decisions and actions are guided by our understanding of truth. If we make decisions based on something other than biblical truth, we'll reap the consequences of that error.

> He underlined the authority of His teaching by reminding listeners that His words were certain and reliable.

Absolute truth is not a popular concept today. Subjectivism, pluralism, and relativism seek to push truth out of the picture. Because much of the world operates without any regard for truth, we must examine what Jesus said was true.

By studying the "amen, amen" sayings of Jesus, we'll be reminded of the unchanging realities of our world. We can study and reflect upon these teachings using a three-step process. Here's how to conduct an "amen, amen" study:

1. Identify the truth statement. Choose one of the twenty-five passages that Jesus begins with the words "amen, amen" from the chart below. After reflecting on the passage, identify the truth that Jesus' words reveal. What does He say is true? Remember to pay careful attention to the overall context of Jesus' statements.

> The truth frees and empowers us to live the kind of life that pleases God.

2. Determine how this truth affects your lifestyle. Just knowing a truth is not enough. We must adjust our lives to truth through practical and concrete application. Spend some time thinking about specific changes you may need to make in response to this truth, and write them down. Though many of these passages are familiar, often we fail to allow the truths they contain to really shape our daily decisions.

3. Identify the world's lie. Jesus' words reveal the lies of the Devil and the world. Almost all of the "amen, amen" statements have a corresponding lie that the Devil has sold to the world. As sure as Jesus reveals the truth, Satan does his best to make us believe a lie. When you reflect on truth, these lies will become clear. Write down the lie that the truth in each passage uncovers so you can remember it when Satan tempts you.

The truth frees and empowers us to live the kind of life that pleases God. Jesus said, "Then you will know the truth, and the truth will set you free." (John 8:32).

Todd D. Catteau is a minister in Denison, Texas.

The "Amen, Amen" Sayings of Jesus

John 1:51; 3:3; 3:5; 3:11; 5:19; 5:24; 5:25; 6:26; 6:32; 6:47; 6:53; 8:34; 8:51; 8:58; 10:1; 10:7; 12:24; 13:16; 13:20; 13:21; 13:38; 14:12; 16:20; 16:23; 21:18

"Amen, Amen" Saying	Truth Statement	Lifestyle Decision	World's Lie
John 12:24: "I tell you the truth, unless a kernel of wheat falls to the ground and dies, it remains only a single seed. But if it dies, it produces many seeds."	Sacrifice produces fruit. Jesus' willingness to give His life has had a profound impact on mankind.	Living a life pleasing to God demands a sacrificial lifestyle. As I give my life, my talents, and my money to others, my life will be multiplied. The fulfilling life is not found in getting what I want, but in giving myself and my resources to others.	The path to satisfaction in the world lies in getting what I want and making myself happy. The rewards and pleasures of this life are all that really matter. Sacrificing my desires for the sake of others' needs is foolishness.

"Amen, Amen" Saying	Truth Statement	Lifestyle Decision	World's Lie
John 13:16: "I tell you the truth, no servant is greater than his master, nor is a messenger greater than the one who sent him."	As servants of Jesus, we are to imitate His example of servanthood.	As Jesus served (i.e., washed feet), we should also serve. Spiritual leadership includes a willingness to meet others' needs in servile ways.	Leadership is not about serving others, but about being served. As a leader, I shouldn't have to perform acts of service that are below me.

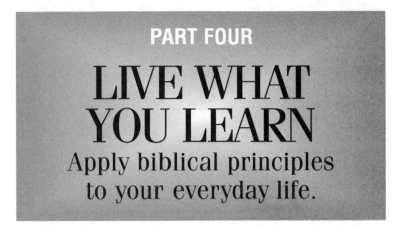

PART FOUR

LIVE WHAT YOU LEARN

Apply biblical principles
to your everyday life.

23

What About You?

Look for personal applications as you study.
JAMES C. GALVIN

After a stressful day at the office and a satisfying dinner, Ed helped Sue wash the dishes and put the children to bed. Later, he sat down in his recliner in the living room, picked up a newspaper and, as usual, turned on the radio to listen to one of his favorite Bible teachers. As he skimmed the paper, he heard the teacher read the text from 1 Samuel 24:1-15.

As Ed listened, the account gripped him. Folding the paper, he picked up his Bible and followed along. As the preacher skillfully explained the story of David's refusal to kill Saul, the king of Israel whom the Lord had anointed, Ed felt he understood what was happening. He wondered what he would learn from this account that he could apply to his own life. At that moment, the preacher concluded, "Neither should we lift up our hands against the Lord's anointed. This is an important thought of crucial significance for us today. Let's pray."

Ed sat up in his recliner. "Wait a minute!" he said, glaring at the radio. "So what? I'm not plotting to assassinate any government leaders! I'm not out to undermine my pastor! What does lifting a hand against the Lord's anointed have to do with me?"

Ed felt cheated. His frustration made him more determined to find out if this passage related to his life. He read the text again and again. No applications came to mind. He pulled two thick commentaries down from his bookshelves but found no answers for his questions. Yet he couldn't shake the feeling that there was something important here for him to know and put into practice. He just didn't know how to get at it. He was stuck.

Perhaps you get stuck like this once in awhile. Some portions of the Bible are difficult to apply. How do you respond when you want to know what to do and cannot find the answer? Where can you go for help when you honestly ask, "So what?"

Application does not always come easily or naturally. Whether or not it does, three important techniques have proved useful for digging personal applications out of puzzling passages. These tools will help you discover the parallels with your own life and know more clearly what you should do about what you learn.

Identify with the People

The first step is to identify with the people in the passage. Granted, the stories in the Bible took place thousands of years ago in a completely different culture. But if you try to understand the people and what they were going through, you will often find connections between their lives and ours. To identify with the people in the passage, ask:

- Who are all of the people involved in the passage?
- How are these people like the people in my world?
- What characteristics in myself do I see represented in these people?

How do you respond when you want to know what to do and cannot find the answer?

Don't forget to include the author and the original audience; they are the people, too. In narrative sections such as Genesis or Matthew, this step is straightforward.

When Ed tried this, he immediately identified with David. Both he and David were men under pressure. David waited patiently for the throne that was rightfully his; Ed was waiting for his long-deserved promotion at work. While Ed could not identify personally with Saul, he couldn't help but notice some similarities between Saul and some men at his office. As he thought about other characters in the story, he saw a parallel between himself and the men who advised David to kill Saul. He had learned to take quick advantage of significant opportunities that arose at work and home. As he was fond of saying, "There are only two kinds of leaders—the quick and the dead."

By asking himself these questions, Ed successfully identified with the people in the story.

Rediscover the Plot

The second tool is to connect what happened in the story with what is happening in your life. To rediscover the plot, ask:

- What is happening in this story or teaching?
- What is the conflict resolution?
- What would I have done in this situation?
- How is this similar to what is happening in my life or in the world today?

Summarizing the plot is an easy way to rediscover it. The questions listed here go further to help you explore the parallels to your own life. The plot is easy to unravel in a gospel or any historical book. But what if a story line is not clearly apparent, as in 2 or 3 John? In this case, check through commentaries and other Bible resources to try to determine the conflict that underlies the passage. Every book in the Bible either contains a story with conflict or speaks directly to one, and understanding this conflict will help unlock additional applications.

The Bible teacher had helped Ed understand what was happening in the passage. Ed now had to find the connections with his own life. A king was not threatening him, nor was he hiding out from any authorities. But as he thought about how this might apply, he realized that his pressure at work was remarkably similar to David's in this story. The manager had been making life difficult for Ed's team and demoralizing the entire division. In the opinion of many workers, Ed was better qualified for the position, and they wanted him to be the manager.

Recently some of Ed's key people had come to him with a plan to undermine the manager in a technically permissible but ethically questionable way. They reasoned that it would be best for the company in the long run if Ed had that position. All week, Ed had felt the pressure to go along with their plan. He was qualified for the position and had been waiting a long time for a promotion. Besides that, he needed the money.

Although the manager was clearly hurting the company, Ed did not feel right about undermining his boss's authority. David's inner turmoil in the story was compelling to him: David was under pressure to get rid of the one man standing between him and what he rightfully deserved. Ed was in a strikingly similar situation—and was about to give in to the pressure from his team. But how could he hold his people back?

Making the Truth Timely

The third step is to transfer the truth in the story from the "then and there" to the "here and now" by identifying the biblical principles in a passage and bringing them into our world. Ask these questions:

- What is the message for all of mankind?
- What is the moral of the story?
- What does this mean for our society and culture?
- How is this relevant to my situation?

You may find one or more transferable principles in each passage in the Bible that you study. These principles are the essence of a passage. Discovering these principles can be as exhilarating as reaching the top of a mountain after a long climb. The view is so inspiring that you might feel tempted to end your journey at the top. But to apply the Bible you must go down the other side, carrying the truth back into daily life. And as the path to the top of the mountain narrows to a single point, but the trails vary on the way down, so each passage will usually have only one meaning, but a wide range of applications.

> An insight from your study of the Bible will not make a difference in your life until you take it personally.

The Bible teacher had correctly identified an important principle from this passage: Do not lift your hand against the Lord's anointed. Ed had to bring this truth to bear on his situation. He decided that his boss may not be anointed, but the Lord had allowed him to be appointed to this position, and it was certainly Ed's duty to be a faithful employee. Any move to get his boss fired or reassigned, even if he didn't break corporate rules, could be considered "lifting his hand against him."

Ed realized in a new way that opportunity does not make a wrong a right. He also knew that if he undercut his boss, he would plant seeds for further dissension in the future and possibly his own undoing. But Ed, a man of action, also knew that doing nothing could mean an intolerably long wait for his own promotion.

He needed to pray for patience and restraint for himself, as well as wisdom to know how to persuade his team to stay in line. He thought, *Perhaps I can tell them of my desire for a position like this and of my appreciation for their confidence in me, but also let them know my convictions about faithfully serving those in authority.*

With David's inspiring example of successfully resisting pressure etched in his mind, Ed began to make some notes for a special meeting in his department.

An insight from your study of the Bible will not make a difference in your life until you take it personally. Bible knowledge alone is insufficient. For a changed life, you also think, pray, and plan to put it into practice. Application is the process of carrying the principles and timeless truths of the Bible back to where you live. I hope you will find these three techniques helpful in applying the Bible to your life. Who knows? They might come in handy as you listen to the radio some night!

James C. Galvin, Ed.D., is vice president of the Livingstone Corporation in Wheaton, Illinois, and one of the senior editors and designers of *The Life Application Bible* (Tyndale House, 1987).

24

Good Fruit

Explore how you can reflect the Holy Spirit's nature.
CINDY HYLE BEZEK

Galatians 5:22-23 is a familiar passage to many of us. In it, Paul describes what a fruitful life looks like: "But the fruit of the Spirit is love, joy, peace, patience, kindness, goodness, faithfulness, gentleness, and self-control."

We'd like to see these qualities in our lives in increasing measure, but it's easy to buzz through the passage like a spiritual grocery list. "I'm not doing too badly on self-control this week, but I am kind of low on patience and gentleness. I guess I need to get more of them. Lord, please make me more patient and gentle today. Amen." Then we leave our Bibles beside our empty coffee mugs and set off on our busy days, no more patient or gentle than we were before our time in the Word.

It's possible, though, to approach the fruit of the Spirit in a way that these traits characterize our lives. We can let our thoughts linger on each character attribute Paul mentions. We can savor the fruit of the Spirit.

Fruitful Character Builders

We can savor the Spirit's fruit by following these steps:

1. Pick a fruit of the Spirit. Prayerfully select the spiritual quality you find most lacking in your life.

2. Define its meaning. Using an ordinary dictionary, look up the fruit you're studying, and record the definition. A Bible dictionary may provide additional insight.

> Eventually you will see Him working more and more of this fruit into your life.

3. Identify synonyms and antonyms. Using a thesaurus, look up the word you're studying, and write down other words that mean the same thing. Now identify the antonyms to the fruit you're studying. (Antonyms are words that mean the opposite of a given word.) Antonyms can give you better understanding of a word because sometimes we understand a concept most clearly by considering what it is not.

4. Identify related words. These will come from the dictionary, the thesaurus, and a Bible concordance. For example, "rejoice," "rejoices," "rejoicing," "rejoiced," "joyous," and "joyful" are all related to joy. A study of joy would be incomplete without examining other related words.

5. Look up Scripture passages that include the word. You'll need a concordance for this. You may also want to look up all the verses that include the synonyms, antonyms, and other words related to that fruit. Write down the verses that are significant to you. This should provide a broad perspective on what the Bible teaches about the character trait you've chosen to study. Take your time with this step. Remember, you want to savor the fruit.

6. Write down your observations. Consider the following questions:

- How do I see this quality in God?
- Why is this quality important to God, to others, and to myself?
- How is this quality cultivated?
- How is this quality hindered?
- What biblical character shows me what this quality looks like in real life?
- What is a key verse about this quality?

> We can let our thoughts linger on each character attribute Paul mentions. We can savor the fruit of the Spirit.

After you think about these questions, you may find that you want to rewrite your definition of the fruit based on what you have learned.

7. Write a summary with a personal application plan. What are the core elements of what you've studied? How can you make this attribute more a part of your life? Distill what you've discovered into a few sentences that can motivate you to put the truths you've learned into practice.

8. Memorize a key verse. Memorization will allow the Holy Spirit to bring this quality to mind at appropriate times in the future. Eventually you will see Him working more and more of this fruit into your life.

9. Choose another fruit. Now that you've finished studying one fruit, it's time to study another. Repeat the process until you've studied all nine.

Once you've completed your study of Galatians 5:22-23, after reading this passage in the future you will linger there, inhaling the sweet fragrance of the attributes of God, marveling that the Holy Spirit is cultivating them in you.

Cindy Hyle Bezek is a freelance writer in Evansville, Indiana.

Getting Personal

Paraphrase Scripture for your daily life.
ANGELA DION

As believers we long to experience God's Word in a rich, personal way. One way to inject new life into your interaction with the Scriptures is to personalize and paraphrase meaningful verses. When we personalize God's Word, we'll see the Scriptures from a new perspective, finding hope and comfort in the trials and joys of everyday life.

Here's a step-by-step method for personalizing Scripture.

Writing Your Paraphrase
To select a verse to paraphrase, consider the following options:

- Has a particular verse been appearing often in your life? Perhaps it addresses an issue God wants you to consider.
- Choose a verse that has been comforting or meaningful to you.
- Select a verse related to a personal struggle, such as anger, worry, pride, or temptation.
- Look through the list of words in a concordance. When a particular subject grabs your attention, choose a verse related to it.

> The purpose of paraphrasing God's Word is to apply it to your situation, not to change the meaning of Scripture or rationalize sin.

Once you've chosen a verse, here's what to do:

1. Read the verse slowly several times. Pay attention to the way it naturally breaks into words and phrases. Write one word or phrase per line in a notebook; then skip two or three lines to allow room for your paraphrase.

2. Proceed with caution. Before you begin paraphrasing a particular passage of the Bible, ask God to help you restate His Word accurately. Pray that you will know and experience the truth of His Word more intimately. Moses warned the Israelites: "Do not add to what I command you and do not subtract from it, but keep the commands of the LORD your God that I give you" (Deuteronomy 4:2). Proverbs 30:6 presents a similar warning: "Do not add to his words, or he will rebuke you and prove you a liar." The purpose of paraphrasing God's Word is to apply it to your situation, not to change the meaning of Scripture or rationalize sin.

Sample Paraphrase

And we know that: I have no doubt, no reservation, or any question that

in all things: in every aspect of this situation—Eric's placement in our home, his departure, our love for him, even my depression and my anger at God—

God works: God is putting His plan into action. It is a work in process. He's been there all along, and He's here with me now.

for the good: His plan is good, upright, and blameless

of those who: for me, my husband, and my son.

love him: We love God unconditionally, not based upon how we feel about this situation.

who have been: We were, are, and continue to be

called: elect, set apart, and chosen of God

according to: because of the fact that

his purpose: God is in control and has a perfect plan, goal, will, and complete foreknowledge of this and all the difficult trials we will ever face.

3. Begin paraphrasing by rewriting each phrase, using your own words. As you do this, personalize the verse to fit your situation. For example, when you see the words "you" or "we" in reference to believers, substitute your name or "me." If words such as "trial" or "sin" relate to your circumstances, describe what you're facing.

As you personalize your verse, use appropriate synonyms for each word. If you're not sure how to restate something, check a thesaurus. Make sure the words flow from one line to the next. You want your final paraphrase to read as a complete thought, not a group of unconnected words and phrases.

4. Meditate on the facets of truth you've discovered. Ask God to show you what He wants you to learn and how to apply it to your life.

A Life-Application Example

A few years ago our family encountered a crisis. After we opened our hearts and home to a foster child for seven months, Eric (who was then a year old) was reunited with his biological father. We had already begun the process of adopting Eric and were devastated when we let him go.

I was depressed following Eric's departure—and angry with God for disappointing my family and me. I had truly believed it was His will for us to adopt the baby.

During this time many friends quoted Romans 8:28 to me: "And we know that in all things God works for the good of those who love him, who have been called according to his purpose." Quite frankly, I got sick of hearing that verse. It meant nothing to me in the pit of my depression and anger.

Nevertheless, God kept bringing it to my attention through well-meaning friends. Instead of feeling more and more resentful each time someone shared this passage of Scripture, I decided to spend time thinking deeply about it. Personalizing this verse for my situation helped me respond in a manner pleasing to God. See page 112 for what I came up with.

Although Eric left our home more than two years ago, I still meditate on this verse. When something reminds me of Eric and threatens to draw me back into depression, I read and reread the insights God gave me as I thought about Romans 8:28. It helps me remember that God is in control, not me.

Personalizing this passage and others has deepened my hunger for Scripture. Likewise, as you paraphrase the verses that have been meaningful to you, your love for God and His Word will grow.

Angela Dion is a freelance writer in Waldorf, Maryland.

> As you paraphrase the verses that have been meaningful to you, your love for God and His Word will grow.

26

What Would You Do?

Decide how to respond in a challenging situation.
EUGENIE L. DANIELS

Are you looking for some meaningful ways to understand and deal with situations in your life? Maybe you are in a rut, and your life feels colorless and barren. Maybe you have experienced a lot of change, and you feel overwhelmed or lost. Maybe you want to start a new ministry, and you need courage and insight. Connecting your story to a biblical story through a Situation Bible Study can provide the empowerment that you need.

Studying the Situation
Bringing your own feelings and situation to the Bible can be like looking into a mirror. You see yourself and your situation more clearly. Then the story can help you decide what direction to take.

1. Spend time thinking about your situation. Ask yourself:

- What does it feel like?
- What docs it remind you of?

For instance, do you feel lost and confused, as if you are in a wilderness? You could study Moses leading God's people through the wilderness in Exodus. If you feel as if you are in a stormy situation, choose Jesus calming the storm in Mark. Many stories in the Bible can help us see God's touch on our lives.

> Several sessions can be spent on one story.

To select an appropriate story, use one from the Bible Stories to Use list shown later, or think of another one that might have a similarity to your situation. If you are doing this study with a new believer who is not familiar with the Bible, you may have to help in the selection.

2. Read your chosen story slowly, reflecting on it. Then ask more questions:

- What is the problem in the story?
- Is it similar to your problem, or is it symbolic of it?

- How do the characters react to the problem?
- Is their reaction similar to yours or are you reacting differently?
- What is God doing in this story? Is He providing something? Is He fulfilling a promise? Is He guiding the characters in a new direction?
- How does God's action in the story relate to what He might do in your life? Has He made promises you can rely on? Will He be leading you in a new direction?

These are the kinds of questions you can begin with as you reflect on the story.

3. Let the story simmer slowly in the back of your mind between readings. Let your story and the biblical story intermingle. Several sessions can be spent on one story. You might take an hour on consecutive Sunday afternoons for the same story.

4. Allow God to speak to you from that story as it simmers in your mind during the week. Summarize how the story applies to your life and God's desire for you in this situation.

Sarah's Example of Barrenness

Before you begin, consider this example of a situation study. Say that life seems monotonous to you, and everything looks gray and barren. You could choose a story of barrenness, such as the story of Abraham and Sarah. Their story would be symbolic of your problem. They were past the years of bearing children, so they thought they could never have a child to fulfill the promise God made to them.

Abraham and Sarah's situation looked absolutely hopeless. In fact, they tried to concoct a solution themselves by substituting Sarah's maid's baby for the child of the promise. You can ask: What is hopeless about your situation? Have you tried to concoct your own solution?

> Bringing your own feelings and situation to the Bible can be like looking into a mirror.

Next, think about Sarah. She actually laughed to herself when she heard the Lord say she would bear a child. Sarah was a skeptic. But God accepted her feelings, even though she lied and said she did not laugh. How do you feel about God delivering you from your situation? You can honestly share your feelings with the Lord.

God made Abraham and Sarah a promise. The promise came true. Has God made promises that you can rely on, too? In Psalm 91, for instance, God has promised to answer when we call upon Him. In Lamentations 3:22 we find the promises that the Lord's love never ceases and His mercies never end.

Nobody would expect Sarah to bear a child at her age, yet God brought new life into a situation where there was no reason to hope. Can you name expectations in your situation? Do your expectations come only from what you can see of your own situation? Can you now hold your barrenness up to God and let Him bring you surprising new life?

Bible Stories to Use

1. Jacob's Dream at Bethel, Genesis 28:10-22
   - When you wonder where God is
   - In times of exile

2. Joseph Interprets Dreams in Prison, Genesis 39:20-41:40
   - When you feel trapped
   - During hard times

3. Elijah and the Famine, 1 Kings 17:1-16
   - When you hunger for something
   - When in need

4. Nehemiah Rebuilds the Wall, Nehemiah 2:1-20
   - When you face a difficult challenge or are trying to rebuild

5. Esther Intercedes, Esther 4:4-5:2
   - When you need courage and strength

6. Jesus Tempted, Matthew 4:1-11
   - When tempted
   - When you question your motivation

7. The Gerasene Demoniac, Mark 5:1-20
   - When you feel fragmented or pulled in many directions

8. A Storm at Sea, Luke 8:22-25
   - During a stormy period
   - When you need training as a disciple

9. Jesus Heals a Blind Man, Luke 18:35-43
   - When you cannot see clearly
   - When you need mercy

10. The Disciples Without the Holy Spirit, Acts 19:1-7
    - During spiritual dryness

—Eugenie L. Daniels

I have used this Bible study method in times of barrenness, separation from family and friends, illness, and when deciding a new course of action. It gives me a new perspective, hope, and direction for dealing with challenging situations in my life.

Eugenie L. Daniels is active in Christian education ministries. One ministry she established connects the children of her church with shut-ins.

Don't Make the Same Mistake

Learn from the unfortunate detours of biblical characters.
CINDY HYLE BEZEK

David's affair. Peter's denial. Noah's drunkenness. Jacob's conniving. God's Word spares no details as it candidly reveals the shortcomings of His children. I'm glad He didn't include my story in His permanent record! But God had a good reason for recording the failures of His faithful ones. Romans 15:4 explains: "For everything that was written in the past was written to teach us, so that through endurance and the encouragement of the Scriptures we might have hope."

Paul expanded upon that idea in 1 Corinthians 10:6,11: "Now these things occurred as examples to keep us from setting our hearts on evil things as they did. . . . These things happened to them as examples and were written down as warnings for us."

God wants us to learn from others to avoid making the same mistakes ourselves.

A Mile in Their Shoes

How can we profit from these failures? One good way is to study the biblical accounts of these people and their actions.

1. Choose a biblical character to study. Perhaps you already have someone in mind, somebody who has always intrigued you or made you ask, "Why did God choose him?" Does it bother you that Abraham lied? That Jonah was a coward? If no one comes to mind, you could look through a book that catalogs Bible characters, such as *Everyone in the Bible* by William P. Barker.

2. Use a concordance to locate every reference to that person. Be sure to include New Testament references to Old Testament characters because these can provide valuable insight. For example, the account of Lot in Genesis mentions little that commends him. But 2 Peter 2:7-8 describes his inner turmoil: "[God] rescued Lot, a righteous man, who was distressed by the filthy lives of lawless men (for that righteous man, living among them day after day, was tormented in his righteous soul by the lawless deeds he saw and heard)."

3. Prayerfully read your character's story several times.

4. Put yourself in that person's shoes and consider these questions:

- What did the character do right? Wrong?
- What motivated him?
- What were the character's moral strengths and weaknesses?
- Was there a clear point at which decline began, or was it gradual?
- What opportunities did he have to repent? How did he respond to these?
- What could the character have done differently to avoid failing God?
- In what way(s) am I like this person?
- What do I need to do to avoid making the same mistakes?

In a spirit of humility, record your observations.

5. Write a summary that includes a personal application plan.

6. Finish your study with a prayer of thanksgiving and praise to God for using "jars of clay" to reveal His all-surpassing power (2 Corinthians 4:7).

> God wants us to learn from others to avoid making the same mistakes ourselves.

Sample Study: Samson

The following is how I completed a study of Samson in Judges 13–16, using the questions listed earlier.

WHAT DID SAMSON DO RIGHT? WRONG?

Samson had godly parents who feared, trusted, and obeyed the Lord. They believed the angel of God who told them their unborn son would deliver Israel from the Philistines. They obeyed all of God's commands concerning how to raise Samson as a Nazirite. The Lord blessed Samson and began to stir in him while he was still living at home with his parents.

But Samson made his first wrong move when he visited the Philistine town of Timnah. In that city, he met and soon married a Philistine woman, even though God had prohibited marriage between His children and the Canaanites (Exodus 34:16; Deuteronomy 7:3). Later Samson visited a Philistine prostitute. Ultimately he allowed Delilah, his Philistine mistress, to rob him of the source of his strength.

Despite these failures, however, the author of Hebrews still included Samson in his list of the Old Testament heroes of the faith (Hebrews 11:32).

WHAT MOTIVATED SAMSON?

Although Samson should have been motivated by God's extraordinary call on his life, he seemed to be compelled by cravings for sensual pleasure and revenge. Even in the final victory in which he slew more than three thousand Philistines, he did not destroy the temple because of the idol worship that was taking place. Instead, he asked God to give him the strength to topple the massive structure to "get revenge on the Philistines for my two eyes" (Judges 16:28).

WHAT WERE SAMSON'S STRENGTHS AND WEAKNESSES?
Samson had unprecedented physical strength, and he acknowledged God as the source of that strength. But Samson was self-willed, impulsive, and impertinent. He told his parents, "I have seen a Philistine woman in Timnah; now get her for me as my wife" (Judges 14:2). He failed to honor them and the Lord regarding his marriage to a Philistine. Samson had other character flaws as well. He had a blazing temper and could sometimes be cruel. Once he tied 300 foxes' tails together with lit torches between them. And strong as he was physically, he couldn't say no to a weeping woman.

WAS THERE A CLEAR POINT AT WHICH SAMSON'S DECLINE BEGAN, OR WAS IT GRADUAL?
Samson's defeat first became apparent outwardly when he visited Philistia and came back demanding a Philistine wife. But I suspect it must have begun earlier than the text records, whenever he first began putting pleasure before God. Why wasn't Samson's first priority seeking God for wisdom about how to defeat the Philistines, since that was God's revealed purpose for his life? Why didn't Samson respect the desires of his godly parents? Did he think he was above moral failure and compromise?

WHAT OPPORTUNITIES DID SAMSON HAVE TO REPENT, AND HOW DID HE RESPOND TO THESE?
God graciously used Samson's sinful alliance with the Philistine woman to accomplish His purposes. "This was from the LORD, who was seeking an occasion to confront the Philistines" (Judges 14:4). But Samson never realized that God had used the unholy union to establish him as Israel's mighty leader.

> I will praise God that He can use even my folly and sin to accomplish His purposes.

This pattern of blindness to God's work in Samson's life can be seen over and over again: when his wife died, when God's Spirit strengthened Samson for mighty acts, when God miraculously supplied a spring of water, when God helped him escape entrapment in Gaza, and when He allowed Samson three opportunities to recognize Delilah's treachery before his ultimate downfall. All of these were occasions of God's mercy and opportunities for Samson to repent. But he did not. Nor does Judges indicate that Samson ever sought forgiveness for his sins against the Lord.

HOW COULD SAMSON HAVE ACTED DIFFERENTLY TO AVOID FAILING GOD?
Samson could have obeyed his parents, honoring their admonition to marry an Israelite. He could have obeyed God concerning intermarriage, not considering himself above God's law. He could have made God's call on his life his first priority. He could have examined his heart and his ways, asking God for wisdom, purity, and an undivided heart to lead Israel. Samson could have asked the Lord to

avenge him rather than taking matters into his own hands. He could have avoided sexual immorality of any kind. Finally, Samson could have fled from Delilah when he saw that she could not be trusted.

In what way(s) am I like Samson?

Samson's most basic flaw seems to be his failure to put God's will above his own. God was forced to work in spite of Samson rather than with his willing cooperation. I wonder what God would have done through this strong man if Samson had been motivated to honor Him instead of being consumed by his own interests and pleasures.

Too often, I, too, am driven by my own desires. I use my God-given gifts and abilities to further my own agenda rather than God's. Do I limit what God will do through me because I want to serve Him on my terms rather than His? Does He have to work in spite of me? These are questions I need to continue thinking about.

What action must I take to avoid repeating Samson's mistakes?

I want to make the prayer of Jesus in the Garden of Gethsemane a regular part of my prayer life: "Not my will, but yours be done" (Luke 22:42). I will seek to use my spiritual gifts for God's purposes and not my own and ask the Lord to search my heart and repent of any sins He reveals. I will also pray for my son, that he will wholeheartedly fulfill God's plan for his life, avoiding the snares of immorality, unholy partnerships, and revenge. Finally, I will praise God that He can use even my folly and sin to accomplish His purposes.

Cindy Hyle Bezek is a freelance writer in Evansville, Indiana.

28

Change Your Life

Read the Bible for personal transformation.
TERRY POWELL

Someone once said, "The purpose of Bible study is transformation, not informa-tion." That maxim expresses God's desire for us as we study His Word. Paul taught Timothy that "the goal of our instruction is love from a pure heart and a good conscience and a sincere faith" (1 Timothy 1:5, NASB). Similarly, James wrote, "Do not merely listen to the word, and so deceive yourselves. Do what it says" (James 1:22). Neither author emphasized the accumulation of knowledge or doctrine as an end in itself.

What follows is a two-step process that has helped me apply truth to my life. The goal of this process is to forge a link between God's Word and the life situa-tions I typically face. After describing each step, I will illustrate it using my study of Matthew 4:1-11.

One: Look at the Big Picture
The first set of questions prompts you to think about your initial response to the passage and helps you identify the major issues in it. Like a metal detector, these questions alert you to treasure buried just beneath the text's surface.

> Like a metal detector, these questions alert you to treasure buried just beneath the text's surface.

1. How does this passage increase my appreciation for God the Father, Jesus Christ, or the Holy Spirit?
2. What encourages me from the passage? Why?
3. What reasons for praising the Lord does the text offer?
4. What areas of sin does the passage warn against?
5. What positive course of action does the text propose?

Two: Connect Content to Context
These questions connect the content of the passage to the context of your daily life. They will help you construct a bridge that links the Word to your relationships and responsibilities.

6. What people or relationships come to mind as I read? Why?

7. In which responsibilities, circumstances, or decisions do I need to apply principles from this passage?

8. What personal needs or issues has the Holy Spirit exposed as I've studied?

9. What hindrances am I likely to face as I seek to apply this passage?

10. What bearing do these verses have upon my prayer life?

11. Do I need someone's help to make changes? If so, with whom should I talk?

12. If I ignore the text's implications for my life, what negative consequences could I experience?

Don't feel obligated to proceed through these questions in a strictly linear manner. And you don't need to answer every one. An answer to one question may naturally lead to another—even if it's out of sequence or in the other section. The following example demonstrates how I moved back and forth between the questions as I considered how to apply a particular passage to my life.

My Bible Study Example

Recently I looked at Matthew 4:1-11. This narrative describes three ways Satan tempted Jesus just before He launched His public ministry. (To familiarize yourself with this encounter, take a moment to read that passage.) Here are my reflections:

I began with question 1: "How does this passage increase my appreciation for God the Father, Jesus Christ, or the Holy Spirit?" My answer: a soaring appreciation for what Jesus experienced. Though Jesus remained sinless, Satan's enticements certainly tested His resolve. As I pondered the way Jesus responded to temptation, Hebrews 4:15-16 came to mind: "For we do not have a high priest who is unable to sympathize with our weaknesses, but we have one who has been tempted in every way, just as we are—yet was without sin. Let us then approach the throne of grace with confidence, so that we may receive mercy and find grace to help us in our time of need."

This passage from Hebrews prompted me to think about question 10: "What bearing do these verses have upon my prayer life?" Jesus' ability to identify with my temptations should motivate me to appeal to Him when I face spiritual struggles. He is not aloof or unable to understand sin's allure but has identified with my weaknesses. Therefore I shouldn't hesitate to pray to Him in my time of need.

Those thoughts led me naturally to question 8: "What personal needs or issues has the Holy Spirit exposed as I've studied?" The Spirit nudged me to stop and pray about a particular temptation that had been dogging me for days. Despite having a lovely wife to whom I have been faithful for twenty-eight years, I acknowledged that I had been struggling with impure thoughts. My prayer life of late had been too superficial in light of that temptation. I realized that if I failed to pray, the consequences could be moral failure and broken relationships (question 12).

Then I returned to question 5: "What positive course of action does the passage propose?" Jesus had prepared Himself for the confrontation with Satan by fasting and praying for forty days. But in the heat of battle, He quoted verses from Deuteronomy directly related to the nature of each temptation. Jesus' example shows us how familiarity with God's truth works in tandem with prayer to reinforce our ability to resist sin.

I also observed how Satan persisted with the Lord, confronting Him three times. *If the Devil persisted with Jesus,* I thought, *he'll probably persist in his attacks on me, too.* I decided I would rely upon the same defensive strategy Jesus had used: prayer and Scripture memorization. Before leaving my desk, I copied two Bible passages onto three-by-five-inch cards to help me do battle: Romans 6:11-14 and 1 Thessalonians 4:3-5. I decided to carry the cards in my shirt pocket for easy access and to memorize the verses over the next two weeks.

I finished by thinking about question 11: "Do I need someone else's help to make changes?" Despite my hesitancy to admit my susceptibility to impure thoughts, I knew that accountability would help me follow through on my Scripture memory. I phoned a close friend, and we scheduled a breakfast appointment. After we talked about what I'd learned from Matthew 4:1-11, my friend agreed to hold me accountable for my Scripture memory and promised to pray for me. We finished our meeting by praying for each other's purity.

> Though asking the right questions is important, ultimately we are dependent on God's Spirit for life change.

As you can see, I moved freely between both sets of questions, identifying the ways I could implement what I'd learned. Depending on the passage of Scripture you're looking at, the potential applications are almost limitless. Let the questions spur you to consider how to apply God's Word to your context.

Finally, we must remember that though asking the right questions is important, ultimately we are dependent on God's Spirit for life change.

Terry Powell is a professor at Columbia International University in Columbia, South Carolina. He is the author of *Lord, Give Me Wisdom* (WinePress).

29

Write to Learn

Try reflective writing for personal growth.
DIANE KULKARNI

Several years ago, in response to what I was reading and studying in the Bible, I began a practice I call reflective writing. This is written meditation in God's presence, a way of keeping track of what I'm discovering as God reveals Himself and His truth. I keep my meditations in bound spiritual journals, which has been an excellent way of tracking my Christian journey.

No matter how much time I devote to reflective writing, each meditation is worth keeping. Over the years as a Christian I've been amazed how clearly God communicates when I make myself available to Him, taking time to focus on His Word and being receptive to His truth.

Learning to Write Reflectively

During my quiet time I sit at Jesus' feet and He teaches me from the Word. Here's how it can work for you:

1. Prepare a spiritual journal to hold your meditations and other entries. Choose one of the following:

- **Spiral notebooks or blank journals.** Use a journal that you can set up chronologically; it will help you track your spiritual journey.
- **Three-ring notebooks.** These can be divided according to the book or topic of study. Supplemental materials can easily be inserted anywhere.
- **File folders.** I find these to be the most flexible, and they are my personal choice. I file each meditation behind the previous entries in the folder. Then at the end of each year, I take the file to a copy center and have the pages bound with a large plastic spiral. It's satisfying to see a new volume on my bookshelf and to occasionally reread past entries to see how God has led me.

2. Arrange at least thirty minutes of uninterrupted time. If you devote these minutes totally to knowing God through His Word, He will bless you.

3. Read the passage and mark it, highlighting the words or phrases that stand out to you. It's also good to make notes in the margins or in your journal to remind you of your first responses to the text.

> This is written meditation in God's presence, a way of keeping track of what I'm discovering as God reveals Himself and His truth.

4. Copy the part of the passage you want to focus on. Allow ample space between phrases or sentences so you can respond in writing.

5. For ten minutes "discuss" on paper what's in the passage. Write the thoughts going through your mind. This is not structured writing. Don't edit or delete insights, questions, problems, or tangents that seem to be off track. Write down everything.

6. Write a summary of what you learned. Here is where you begin to organize your thoughts. But this, too, should be written down as you are thinking. Don't worry about the structure.

A Workshop Sample Study

The following is an example of a summary one of my workshop participants wrote on Matthew 11:28-30:

> *When I read verse 28, it's easy to recognize that I am the weary and burdened one, but just how do I really "come" to Jesus so that I can have the promised rest? Verse 29 tells me that to "come" is to take His yoke upon me. The question now becomes, how do I take His yoke upon me?*

The questions as I am writing become progressive, one leading into the other. It later becomes obvious to me that the verses were given by God to raise these questions in my mind. And then He answered them for me in profound simplicity. What I try to make complicated, He leads to truth.

> *In verse 30 I found the way: Jesus says that I am to turn away from my burdens and weariness—which could be described as hard and dark, the opposite of easy and light. I am to wear His yoke, which is getting into the harness with Him. In this way, I learn from Him, experience Him, receive rest. Jesus is the light of the world. In Him there is no darkness. So getting close to Him drives my darknesses out of hiding and the burden is lifted. Perhaps the way to "come and take my yoke upon you" is simply to surrender. I stop controlling, and instead trust His lordship and faithfulness. I submit.*

—RANDI HUNSAKER

7. Include creative writing ideas or research decisions. After completing the previous steps, you may want to try writing a poem, a song, or a creative essay on what God shows you. Or perhaps your meditation caused something to surface and you need to further study or research for answers. For example, Randi's conclusion about surrender could lead her to a word study on surrender, or to read a book on the subject. Include in your notebook either your piece of writing, or what you intend to research.

8. Be receptive to God's truth. Over the days following the initial meditation on a passage, I choose to be receptive to what God will show me that underscores His truth and its applications. When this happens, I write it down. I often clip news articles, magazine pictures, sermon portions, famous quotes, and even cartoons to add to my journal. These are exciting connections with what God is teaching. Poetry, essays, and other projects have grown from my meditations. As I continue to revise these works, God takes me even deeper into the meaning of the passages to bless me again and again.

> As I continue to revise these works, God takes me even deeper into the meaning of the passages to bless me again and again.

Diane Kulkarni is a freelance writer. She is active in her local church as a women's Bible study leader and as the editor of her church newsletter.

30

Think on These Things

Expand your understanding with biblical meditation.
MIKE HILDEBRAND

The psalmist wrote, "Oh, how I love your law! I meditate on it all day long" (Psalm 119:97). And we read in Psalm 1:1-2, "Blessed is the man . . . [whose] delight is in the law of the LORD, and on his law he meditates day and night." When many of us hear the word "meditation," we think of quiet reflection upon God. But does that constitute biblical meditation? If we were to peek around the corner and catch the Old Testament believer in the act of meditation, what would we see?

A better question might be, "What did meditation sound like?" We tend to consider meditation an introspective and silent experience. But the Old Testament Jewish meditator cried out to *Yahweh* (Psalm 55:17) and voiced his complaint to God (Psalm 64:1). In both of these passages the Hebrew term *siyach* is used. *Siyach* is one of two words that we find translated as "meditate" in our English Bibles.

In fact, both Hebrew words for "meditate" in the Old Testament (*siyach* and *hawgaw*) carry the idea of vocalization. The word *siyach* is defined as "to ponder," but it can also mean "to converse aloud." The primary meaning of *hawgaw* (Joshua 1:8; Psalm 1:2; 19:14; 77:12; 143:5) is to make a low sound, such as the moaning of a dove (Isaiah 38:14) or the growling of a lion (Isaiah 31:4). The English equivalent is "to mutter."

Asaph's Noisy Meditations

Biblical meditation was almost always a noisy affair. In Psalm 77, Asaph provides us an example of what meditation looked like. Though we never discover what was troubling him, the intensity of his struggle is clear. In Psalm 77, he uses both *siyach* and *hawgaw* as he pours out his anguish to God.

Asaph's initial meditation in verses 1-6 is introspective and self-focused: "I cried out to God for help; I cried out to God to hear me. When I was in distress . . . my soul refused to be comforted. I remembered you, O God, and I groaned; I mused [*siyach*], and my spirit grew faint. . . . I remembered my songs in the night. My heart mused [*siyach*] and my spirit inquired."

Asaph's first conclusion after venting his distress is negative and irrational: "Has God forgotten to be merciful?" (verse 9).

Asaph didn't stop, however, at simply voicing his doubts to God through his groaning and crying. After his first meditation, Asaph meditated again, this time turning his soul's attention to God's mighty deeds. "I will meditate [*hawgaw*] on all your works and consider [*siyach*] all your mighty deeds" (verse 12). This meditation is focused upon God. Instead of doubt, Asaph's second meditation leads to reassurance.

Asaph practiced biblical meditation by turning his attention to God and His "mighty deeds." Even when he moaned and groaned to God in self-absorbed depression, he was meditating. But it was only as he turned his attention to God that he found reassurance.

Biblical meditation is interactive and expressive. It is the subjective aspect of understanding the Word of God. By meditating, we make the correlation between the things God is saying and the joys and pains

> **Biblical meditation was almost always a noisy affair.**

of our lives. It is different from the analyses and exegetical exercises we generally include in our Bible study. Meditation allows God's Word to connect with our lives in a way that enables application.

Meditation in the New Testament

The New Testament has no exact equivalent of either *siyach* or *hawgaw*. However, a parallel is seen in such statements as "pray continually; give thanks in all circumstances" (1 Thessalonians 5:17-18) and "do not be anxious about anything, but in everything . . . present your requests to God" (Philippians 4:6).

We tend to look at prayer and meditation as separate disciplines. In reality, they are two dimensions of the same spiritual exercise. In what other relationship would it make sense to conduct a conversation with fifteen minutes of listening, followed by fifteen minutes of speaking? Meditation is simply speaking and listening to God by expressing what's on our hearts and reflecting upon His Word in the same exercise.

Developing the Habit

The following steps will help you integrate meditation into your relationship with God.

1. Pray out loud. When your heart is heavy, pour your heart out to God by praying aloud. You might couple this activity with a walk. How well I remember some of those walks when I was a very young believer. It seemed that I had more than my share of problems—feelings of inadequacy, struggles with sin, and fears of failing as a Christian. I would be encouraged with my quiet time in the morning, but by evening I was usually overwhelmed by my lack of faith in God.

2. Connect your prayer to the Scriptures. By God's grace, I had developed the habit of Scripture memory. After dinner I would walk through my neighborhood and talk to God about the issues I faced. At the same time, I would think about a verse and how it might relate to what was on my mind. You might want to choose a verse that God has impressed upon your heart recently, or one that directly applies to your situation.

3. Write out your meditations by keeping a journal. Journaling our thoughts, burdens, and prayers is another form of meditation. If this is a new idea for you, consider this simple format:

- **List a few things you might be facing:** new opportunities, trying circumstances, challenging relationships, issues with your children.

- **Address God when you write.** Jesus told us to address God as our Father when we pray. Instead of writing, "Finances are tight," write, "Father, the financial pressure we're facing right now is getting me down."

- **Read a portion of Scripture** from your reading program or perhaps from Psalms. If a passage speaks to you, write the verse in your journal.

- **Relate the passage to the personal issue.** Again, address your Father when you write. If you read Hebrews 13:5, don't write, "Contentment is good." Instead write, "Father, I think You're saying that I'm not content."

- **Tell God how you feel.** "Father, it's hard to be content when we're two months behind on our mortgage payment and we can't see how or when we'll be able to get caught up. But Father, You promise that You will never fail me or forsake me." The keys are to keep looking at the Scriptures and to keep writing.

> Biblical meditation is turning to our heavenly Father in His Word and making sure that our thoughts are influenced by His thoughts.

- **Pray through the psalms with a friend.** This kind of meditation is especially important when you are discouraged or angry. Here are tips to make this work for you.

  a. **Select a psalm related to the problem you're facing.** If no psalm comes immediately to mind, begin with the psalm that corresponds to the date; then read them in intervals of thirty. For example, if today is July 16, you would read Psalms 16, 46, 76, 106, and 136.

  b. **Alternate reading and praying.** I like to begin by praying, "Open my eyes that I may see wonderful things in your law" (Psalm 119:18). Then read a verse or two out loud and pray the verse back to the Lord, personalizing as you pray. For example, Psalm 16:1. "Keep me safe, O God, for in you I take refuge," becomes, "Father, thank You that even though I don't have enough money to pay all my bills this month, I am still safe because of You." Then your friend reads on and stops to pray in the same way.

   c. Look for what the passage says about God. It's easy to read the
      Bible looking for principles rather than what God says is true about
      Himself and His purposes.

Connecting the Message to Our Lives

Meditation connects the message of God with the realities in our lives in a way
that the other Word-centered disciplines do not. It brings God "into the loop."
Biblical meditation is turning to our heavenly Father in His Word and making sure
that our thoughts are influenced by His thoughts. Let us pray with the psalmist,
"May the words of my mouth and the meditation of my heart be pleasing in your
sight, O LORD, my Rock and my Redeemer" (Psalm 19:14).

Mike Hildebrand serves on The Navigators staff in Phoenix, Arizona.

31

Storing Up

Memorize the Word for daily encouragement.
DAVID ROBINSON

Two years ago, my wife and I bought a forested lot on the Oregon coast. When we first walked on the property, we discovered a huge spruce tree, twelve feet across at the forest floor, with roots running down into a stream nearby and a trunk reaching up hundreds of feet. I sat at the foot of its trunk and prayed, "Lord, make me like this tree, just as You promised in Psalm 1, as I meditate upon Your Word day and night."

Memorizing Scripture has been a regular part of my spiritual growth for many years. Two passages from Psalms describe why this discipline is vital to our lives. The first is: "Blessed is the man . . . [whose] delight is in the law of the LORD, and on his law he meditates day and night. He is like a tree planted by streams of water, which yields its fruit in season and whose leaf does not wither. Whatever he does prospers" (Psalm 1:1-3). The second is: "I have hidden your word in my heart that I might not sin against you. . . . I remember your ancient laws, O LORD, and I find comfort in them. . . . I will never forget your precepts, for by them you have preserved my life" (Psalm 119:11,52,93). According to these verses, Scripture memory will make our lives fruitful, guard us from sin, comfort us in times of sorrow, and preserve us.

Over the years I've tucked away dozens of key verses that God has used to produce fruitfulness in my life. The more I've memorized, the more I've desired to hide larger portions of His Word in my heart—even an entire book of the Bible. Though it took me more than ten years to work up the courage, last summer I memorized the book of James, a letter of 107 verses.

A year later, passages from James continue to permeate my thinking, enabling me to bear fruit in specific situations I face daily. I've found my mind more attentive to the leading of the Holy Spirit and my heart more tender and obedient. When I'm confronted with a critical or judgmental person, James 4:12 asks me, "Who are you to judge your neighbor?" Then James reminds me, "Mercy triumphs over judgment" (James 2:13), and I find myself responding more compassionately. Recently, when a sick church member called me, James 5:15-16 led me to go with an elder to pray over him: "And the prayer offered in faith will make the sick person well; the Lord will raise him up. . . . The prayer of a righteous man is powerful and effective."

Steps to Memorizing a Book

Memorization is a mental skill that can be developed through practice. Though it may seem like an intimidating goal, you can memorize an entire book of the Bible. Here are a few guidelines I've found helpful.

1. Select a book of the Bible that has consistently refreshed you and helped you grow in your faith. Sometimes passages from a particular book speak deeply and repeatedly to us throughout our walk with God. These books become the root systems for our faith. Paul used this metaphor to describe the kind of faith we're to have: "So then, just as you received Christ Jesus as Lord, continue to live in him, rooted and built up in him, strengthened in the faith as you were taught, and overflowing with thankfulness" (Colossians 2:6-7).

2. Set a date to complete your memorization project. Generally, a chapter a month is a reasonable goal. Thus, a shorter book could be memorized in a season, whereas a longer book might take a year. When we give ourselves a goal, we can begin to take smaller steps to arrive at that destination.

> Scripture memory will make our lives fruitful, guard us from sin, comfort us in times of sorrow, and preserve us.

3. Chart your course. Break up the amount of time you've committed to the entire task into smaller units, and set specific mini-goals to be reached within each leg of the journey. For example, I committed to memorize James over a summer but set little goals of memorizing half a chapter every two weeks and at least a verse a day. You might want to mark these minigoals in your Bible margins in pencil or create a chronological checklist to mark your progress and keep you on schedule.

It's important to create a system that works for you and provides some structure to the memorization process. Without such a plan, the task can seem overwhelming, and you'll be more tempted to give up.

4. Begin memorizing. For most people, memorization is difficult mental work. Perhaps because of our increasingly technological culture, we don't memorize information as much as previous generations did. We need to relearn the steps required for this work. I've found that a four-step process helps me memorize most efficiently:

- Read the sentence out loud.
- Recite the sentence from memory.
- Review the sentence mentally.
- Recite the sentence from memory.

5. Repeat this cycle until you're able to recite the sentence from memory easily and with consistent accuracy. Once the sentence is memorized, go on to the next sentence, using the same process, sentence by sentence, verse by verse, until you've worked through the entire book.

6. Carry your Bible with you and work on memorization through the day. I carry my pocket Bible with me everywhere and work on memorizing new verses during idle moments. Our days are filled with many little spaces during which we can memorize, such as waiting at a red light or standing in line at a store. I've found it easier to memorize sentences and paragraphs a little at a time throughout a day rather than trying to cram a lot into my brain all at once.

> It's important to create a system that works for you and provides some structure to the memorization process.

7. Memorize with others, if possible. I meet weekly with several other believers. Among other things, we share the passages we've been memorizing. Working on Scripture memory with other people provides both account-ability and encouragement to press on. Why not gather a few friends together weekly or monthly and recite the verses you've been learning? Combining community with memorization makes hiding God's Word in our hearts a more encouraging process.

By memorizing a book of the Bible, I am becoming more and more like that majestic spruce, strong and flexible, growing toward heaven while reaching out to a world in need. God's Word planted deeply into our memories can help all of us become more fruitful people in our daily lives.

David Robinson is author of the parenting book *The Family Cloister: Benedictine Wisdom for the Home* (N.Y.: Crossroad, 2000). He serves as pastor of Community Presbyterian Church, Cannon Beach, Oregon.

32

Praying the Psalms

Recite God's poetry for effective intercession.
CATHY MILLER

If you usually approach Bible study as an academic challenge, add variety to your time in God's Word by praying through the book of Psalms. Because many of the psalms were originally written as prayers, they give expression to our own hearts' cries. Try this method for one month, in addition to your regular Bible study. You will find encouragement and practical help as God reaches out to you through His written Word.

1. Start with prayer. Ask God to open your heart as you open His Word. Come into His presence with a thankful and expectant attitude.

2. Pick a psalm for the day. Each day for a month, read the psalm that corresponds with the day's date. For example, if you start on the first day of the month, read Psalm 1. When you pray the psalms a second time, start where you left off.

> Because many of the psalms were originally written as prayers, they give expression to our own hearts' cries.

3. Use your pencil. As you read the day's psalm, underline phrases that catch your eye. Circle words that make the text meaningful to you. Mark verses that apply to your own life in specific ways.

4. Dig deeper. Look up cross-references for the verses you've marked. Read the related passages. Resist the temptation to pull out your reference books or Bible commentaries. During this devotional time, let God speak to you through His Word alone.

5. Ask questions. Spend a few minutes wondering about what you've read. Bring your honest questions to God in prayer.

- How does this passage relate to me?
- Is there something about my life that You want to me to change?
- What hope can I find in these verses?

6. Hide a verse in your heart. Choose one verse, or part of a verse, from your daily psalm to memorize. The words that you tuck away in your heart will show up in wonderful ways in your daily life.

7. Pray your verse. Pray your memory verse for yourself or for someone else. For example: "Father, I pray that Christina would delight in Your Word and think about it day and night." "Lord, the pull of the world is so strong! Please draw Christina close to You during her teenage years. Help me not to fret, but to trust You."

> Pour out your heart to God, just as the psalmists did. Be transparent and real with Him.

Pour out your heart to God, just as the psalmists did. Be transparent and real with Him. He knows everything about you, and He loves you!

8. Note the answers. When God answers your request, make a note of it next to your dated prayer.

Reviewing your shorthand prayers and God's answers will encourage you to continue praying daily through the book of Psalms. After you have prayed through the psalms, use the same approach with Proverbs or the Epistles. You'll be blessed!

Cathy Miller leads a Neighborhood Bible Studies group. She also supports her husband as he leads a surfers' Bible study.

Notes

Chapter One

1. Charles Simeon, "Evangelical Preaching" in *Classics of Faith and Devotion* (Sisters, Ore.: Multnomah).
2. John Stott, *Between Two Worlds,* USA edition (Grand Rapids, Mich.: Eerdmans, 1981).

Chapter Two

3. Gordon D. Fee and Douglas Stuart, *How to Read the Bible for All Its Worth* (Grand Rapids, Mich.: Zondervan, 1993), p. 35.
4. Fee, Stuart, p. 35.
5. Fee, Stuart, p. 35.
6. Fee, Stuart, p. 35.

Chapter Three

7. Harper Collins, ed., *Funk and Wagnall's Standard Desk Dictionary* (San Francisco: Harper Trade, 1984).
8. Howard Marshall with A. R. Millard and D. R. Wood, *New Bible Dictionary* (Downers Grove, Ill.: InterVarsity, 1996).
9. William E. Vine, *Expository Dictionary of Bible Words* (Grand Rapids, Mich.: Zondervan, 1985).
10. *The NIV Study Bible Tenth Anniversary Edition* (Grand Rapids, Mich.: Zondervan, 1995), p. 3.
11. *The NIV Study Bible*, p. 24.

Chapter Eight

12. Tyron Edwards, D.D., ed., *The New Dictionary of Thoughts* (StanBook, Inc., 1977), p. 740.

Chapter Eighteen

13. Gordon D. Fee and Douglas Stuart, *How to Read the Bible for All Its Worth* (Grand Rapids, Mich.: Zondervan, 1993), p. 82.

BIBLICAL STUDIES FOR PRACTICAL LIVING.

Discipleship Journal Bible Studies

Based on excerpts from top *Discipleship Journal* articles, these eight studies help readers go beyond just gaining knowledge to experiencing real growth and change:

Beating Busyness—Identify and tackle stressful issues in your life.

Becoming More Like Jesus—Understand Jesus' teachings on character and live them out.

Building Better Relationships—Develop deeper sensitivity, love, and loyalty in all of your relationships.

Following God in Tough Times—Find out how to accept and gain perspective of life's difficult circumstances.

Growing Deeper with God—Learn to interact with God on a personal level.

Nurturing a Passion for Prayer—Discover what true communication with God is all about.

Redeeming Failure—Learn to deal with regret and move beyond blame.

Your Money and Your Life—Find balance between the good and the bad of wealth.

To get your copies, visit your local bookstore, call 1-800-366-7788, or log on to www.navpress.com. Ask for a FREE catalog of NavPress products. Offer #BPA.

NAVPRESS

BRINGING TRUTH TO LIFE

www.navpress.com